Laughing Through the Years
A New Treasury of Jewish Humor

Laughing Through the Years

A New Treasury of Jewish Humor

RETOLD BY DAVID C. GROSS

Walker and Company
New York

Library of Congress Cataloging in Publication Data
Gross, David C., 1923–
Laughing through the years: a new treasury of Jewish
humor / retold by David C. Gross.
p.   cm.
"A Walker large print original"—T.p. verso.
ISBN 0-8027-2657-7
1. Jewish wit and humor.   2. Large type books.
I. Title.
[PN6231.J5G67   1991]
808.8'82'089924—dc20   91-3120
CIP

A Walker Large Print Original
Published by Walker and Company, 720 Fifth Avenue,
New York, New York 10019

Published simultaneously in Canada by Thomas Allen &
Son Canada, Limited, Markham, Ontario

Printed in the United States of America

2   4   6   8   10   9   7   5   3   1

For Esther

Weep before God, and laugh before people.
—YIDDISH PROVERB

Even in laughter, the heart aches.
—BOOK OF PROVERBS

Contents

Acknowledgments

Many people—friends, relatives, unknown authors, and nodding acquaintances—flooded me with stories when it became known that I was working on this book. Some of their stories were too linguistic; that is, they were based on twists and turns of the Hebrew or Yiddish languages, and sometimes of what is now known as "Yinglish." Other stories were unusable because they were far too raw for this volume.

I do wish to thank a few people whose sense of Jewish humor will certainly add to people's enjoyment and laughter: Florence and Bernard Rosenberg, Dr. Leon Rosenberg, Paula Spector, Miriam Cogan, Seymour Sandos, and the late Rolf Bergman.

Preface

Many complex factors—religious, political, historical, cultural—helped to sustain the Jews through nearly two thousand years of exile. That is, from the time of the destruction of the Holy Temple in Jerusalem by the Romans, in the year 70, until the reestablishment of the State of Israel in 1948, Jews have lived on sufferance among non-Jews . . . a period of nearly two thousand years.

True, many Jews in many parts of the world have become part and parcel of the countries in which they have resided, and do not believe that they are in exile or that anyone is doing them a favor by allowing them to enjoy full rights. Certainly that is true in the United States and in the Western countries where democracy rules.

But equal rights for Jews and full citizenship are phenomena that date back only some two hundred years, roughly to the time of the French Revolution. Previously, in country after country in Europe, Asia, and North Africa, Jews were permitted to remain if their services were needed, but the moment they were not—or if it was expedient to expel

Jews so as to placate a mob, or if a local nobleman believed that an easy way out of his financial indebtedness to Jews would be expulsion or massacre—then expulsion or massacre was very often the path taken.

And yet, despite pogroms, expulsions, forced conversions, and restrictions on where they could reside and what kind of work they could do, the Jews carried on, determined to maintain a way of life that they believed to be good, serving God, and bringing in its wake serenity and inner fulfillment.

One of the reasons that they succeeded in doing so was that they gradually, over a period of years, developed a finely honed sense of humor. The comic David Steinberg puts it well: "The Jews always felt themselves to be outsiders, looking in on an imperfect world, from which they are excluded." Much of Jewish humor, when carefully dissected, is really universal humor, but there are also certain stories, certain ways of looking at life, certain perspectives that are decidedly Jewish. One comic analyst said Jewish humor sits on a sad past and looks at life through a prism of paradox and self-derision.

To put it another way: The Torah, the Jewish Bible, or for that matter, all of Jewish religious teaching, is painfully honest and truthful. All the great biblical personalities are presented as they really are, with their pluses and minuses; nothing is omitted, so that the truth will emerge. In Jewish humor, a similar attitude is taken—life is confronted with a mixture of almost ruthless candor and sharp, Talmudic reasoning, and what emerges is funny—especially the ability to laugh at oneself.

Through Jewish humor, we see a rich, complex tapestry of real life.

It is no accident that so many comedians are Jewish—it is as though they were born with an extra, Jewish chromosome (which of course they are not). Jack Benny, Mel Brooks, Milton Berle, Henny Youngman, Buddy Hackett, Alan King, Sid Caesar, Jackie Mason, and so many more—all these funny men are Jewish. For many, humor has been a wonderful weapon with which to climb higher on the social ladder. For some, humor is a weapon useful in fighting off a hostile world.

When people can laugh together, they won't fight each other. Was there ever anything more beautiful than seeing the late, great Jewish comic, Danny Kaye, on behalf of the United Nations Children's Fund, making children of many colors and races and backgrounds, who did not share a common language, laugh uproariously together?

Perhaps prospects for the world would improve if every nation would insist that their government include a Minister of Humor.

Some of the stories that follow actually happened, while most are the figment of someone's imagination. Some stories are found in Yiddish anthologies, most of them now out of print. Other stories spring up in response to events of the day, and somehow, quite incredibly, travel across the country and across the world, often in a matter of days.

For example: at the start of the Persian Gulf crisis, the story goes, President Bush—at the suggestion of his advisers, who said that Moses could guide the White House in upcoming desert warfare—told his secretary to get Moses on the phone. The telephone operator tried and tried, and finally decided to try the Israeli prime minister, Yitzhak Shamir.

When told that President Bush was "burning up the wires" trying to get hold of Moses, the Israeli leader at first refused to take the White House call. Finally, however, he relented, and when Bush spoke to him, Shamir explained:

"Mr. President, your operator said President Bush was burning up the wires, trying to get hold of Moses. So at first I refused to accept the call—you see, the last time we had an episode of a 'burning bush,' we had to wander in the desert for forty years."

Within days of the outbreak of Persian Gulf hostilities, the story was being told in New York, California, Jerusalem, London, and elsewhere. How? Nobody really knows.

Enjoy!

Laughing Through the Years
A New Treasury of Jewish Humor

◆◆◆◆◆◆◆◆◆◆◆ **1** ◆◆◆◆◆◆◆◆◆◆◆

In America, the Golden Land

Although the United States of America continues to change almost hourly, presenting one face to the world in the morning and another in the evening, it is still head and shoulders, above all, the quintessential Golden Land. Native-born Americans often do not realize just how much America means to underprivileged people in the four corners of the world. From the moment the first Jews arrived in what was to become America—back in 1654—they knew that the United States was the Golden Land, and they cherished their good fortune in living in America.

Florida Encounter

Jacob Goldstein had never really had a vacation, although he had been working hard for more than forty-five years. One wintry, windy morning he

1

flew out of Chicago, headed for the sunny climate of Florida. When he stepped down onto the Sunshine State's soil, he could not believe the contrast between Chicago's icy weather and Miami's warm, sunny ambience.

Now in his late sixties, Jacob had recently lost his wife; his two children were grown and well established, one son living in Boston and the younger one in Dallas. As Jacob walked toward the airport exit he noticed a rather beautiful young woman—she could not have been more than thirty—who smiled at him as he walked by, and approached him politely. Her smile lit up her face as she whispered to him, "I'm selling."

For a moment he did not understand. Then he realized what she was offering, and what kind of woman she was. And yet, he was lonely and alone and she looked so pretty. He smiled, she took his arm, and they went off together, directly to the hotel where he had booked a reservation.

Two weeks later, Jacob Goldstein feared that he had contracted a terrible disease, and blamed it on his unusual encounter with the woman at the airport. He visited a local physician, who confirmed that he had indeed contracted a sexually transmitted illness, but assured him that it was a mild case and that it could be cured easily and fully. In ten days' time, the symptoms disappeared and Jacob felt fine and was also very grateful. He spent the rest of his vacation basking in the sun, playing golf, and making new friends. He returned home to Chicago rested.

One year later, Goldstein flew down to Miami again, in search of warm weather. At the airport he walked along toward the exit, and when he saw the same young woman of the year before, he approached her and said in a low voice: "So, what are you selling now? Cancer?"

Snow Knife

Buddy Hackett likes to tell about when he lived for a time in northern New Jersey. Not exactly svelte in appearance, he has had a lifelong battle with being overweight. One night, in the course of a strenuous three-week diet, he awoke in the middle of the night, unable to control his desire to eat. Leaving his wife asleep, he tiptoed downstairs, opened the refrigerator, took out a half-eaten salami, sliced off a half-dozen pieces, placed them between two slices of rye bread, and in the still of the night began to eat.

Suddenly, while he was chewing, he realized that he had just committed a terrible mistake. His wife maintained a kosher kitchen, separating meat from dairy dishes. And Buddy had just sliced the salami with a knife designated solely for dairy foods. He looked at the knife, smeared with ketchup, resting innocently on the counter, and out of the blue the solution to his dilemma presented itself. He remembered an ancient custom that was resorted to in such cases: a knife that had been made unkosher could be salvaged and made kosher again by plunging it into the soil, and then washing it thoroughly.

Still dressed in pajamas and a robe, and his feet in a pair of scuffs, Buddy grabbed the offending

3

knife, which had a rather longish blade, opened the door of his home, stepped outside to the lawn, which was covered with a newly fallen layer of soft snow, and began plunging his ketchup-dripping knife into the soil. Without any warning, he heard a loud voice not more than twenty feet away: "Freeze! Keep your hands up! Don't move! Drop the knife!"

It took two hours for Buddy to convince the police, who had been patrolling the area, that a knife was being made kosher and that there was no body on the lawn, and that the red ooze on the blade was ketchup and not blood. Of course, his wife did not speak to him for the next two weeks, although he resumed his diet with renewed commitment.

Second Chance

Mimi Horowitz worked as a secretary for a large clothing firm on New York's Seventh Avenue, often called "Fashion Avenue." She was pretty enough, in her late twenties, and perhaps too choosy—her greatest ambition, shared with her widowed mother with whom she lived, was to land a suitable husband.

One day she returned from work, her eyes red from crying. "Mama," she called out as soon as she entered the apartment, "I'm pregnant—please, don't get excited; it's my boss. You remember, we went to a convention in Las Vegas a few months ago? Well, anyway, I don't know what to do now!" She began to sob uncontrollably, while her mother

4

patted her shoulders and simultaneously vowed she would give her daughter's boss a piece of her mind.

The next morning, while Mimi took the day off, the mother came charging into the office of her daughter's employer. "Nu!" ("Well!") she shouted at him, when she entered his office. "What's going to be?"

The elegantly clad employer, a handsome and unmarried man in his mid-thirties, held up his hand. "Please, take a seat, Mrs. Horowitz," he said. "I'm making all the arrangements. Mimi will have the best doctor money can buy before the baby is born, and she'll stay in the best hospital, and later, after she gives birth, I'm arranging for a trust fund for her and the baby—she'll receive a lifelong weekly check for one thousand dollars."

Mrs. Horowitz was taken aback. She was struck dumb by what her daughter's employer had just promised. Finally she opened her mouth, and in a whisper said, "Tell me, God forbid, if she has a miscarriage, you'll give her a second chance?"

Yiddish Gentile

One Sabbath afternoon a newly arrived immigrant from the old country was strolling in Central Park, New York. He was startled to see a man seated on a bench, puffing on a cigar, and reading the Yiddish paper. The newcomer turned to his companion and said, "What a country this is! Even the Gentiles here can read Yiddish!"

5

Odessa Revenge

A traveling salesman from New York, who still retained a Yiddish accent, was inured to the anti-Semitic taunts he received from local buyers. Once, when he was in Alabama selling twine to a department store buyer, the southerner said he would buy some twine from him, but only as much "as reaches from the top of your Jewish nose to the tip of your circumcised penis." The salesman nodded, and noted the order in his order pad.

Two weeks later a shipment containing nine hundred cartons of twine arrived at the southern store. A note was attached: "Thanks for your generous order. Invoice follows." The memo was signed, Jacob Feldstein, living in New York, circumcised in Odessa.

Winning Pies

A newly arrived immigrant from Poland was taken to the Automat in New York, and handed a fistful of nickels. His cousin left him alone for ten minutes, and when he returned saw that the newcomer kept pushing nickels into the apple pie slot.

"Moishe," the American yelled at him. "Enough already—look, you got already six pieces of apple pie."

The immigrant responded, "Why do you care if I keep on winning?"

One Less

At the turn of the century, a funeral procession on the Lower East Side passes the plant of one of the popular Yiddish dailies. A printer is looking out the window at the cortege, when he spots his brother-in-law, one of the mourners. "Print one less," the mourner calls out.

Immigrant Successes

Three Jewish immigrants arrived in the United States soon after the end of the First World War. All three were uneducated, unmarried, and determined to succeed in America, the great land of opportunity. They had been friends, classmates, and neighbors in the old country, and now they sat in a Lower East Side cafeteria, saying good-bye to one another.

One of them, David Goldsmith, had a cousin in Chicago who urged him to come to the Windy City, where he would help him get started. Joseph Silverstein had a relative in St. Louis who also urged him to relocate, promising to help him. Only Isaac Schneider had no relatives in the U.S., and so he decided to remain in New York. The three friends vowed eternal devotion to one another and pledged that they should meet again in the same cafeteria, in twenty-five years.

A quarter of a century has now passed, and the three men meet again in the restaurant. All three look prosperous, and can't wait to tell one another about the last twenty-five years. Goldsmith explains first: "You know, I didn't know what to do, so I decided to try the gold business because of my name. I was just plain lucky! I became a rich man." Then Silversmith recounted that "the same thing happened to me—because of my name I went into the silver business, and it was a lucky break for me. Thank God, I do very well!"

Schneider smiled. "You know, my name means 'tailor' so I decided to become a tailor—it's an honest living. I became an apprentice, I learned the trade, and after five years I opened my own store. I called it 'Taylor's' and spelled it with a *y,* to be a little fancy. But business was terrible, just awful. I couldn't pay the rent, I didn't know how to bring in customers so I could work and earn something. One day, I was in synagogue, I was praying, and I made a *neder,* a solemn vow, if God will help me in my business, I'll give half the profits to Him. And then like a miracle, business picked up, I hired more people, I opened new shops, we expanded into retailing, and now, thank God, I do very well. Maybe you heard of my chain of stores? I call it Lord and Taylor's."

Oriental Yiddish

On the Lower East Side there is a kosher Chinese restaurant. One afternoon a family visiting from Montreal enjoys dinner there. As the father is paying his bill, he asks the cashier-owner, "Tell me, how did you get the Chinese waiter to speak such a good Yiddish?"

"Sh, sh," the owner whispers, "he thinks he's talking English."

Theatrical Demise

There are some people who swear that the following actually happened. A melodrama was playing in one of the popular Yiddish theaters that flourished on New York's Second Avenue during the 1920s and 1930s. In one particular torrid scene, the leading male actor suddenly suffered a heart attack. In front of nearly one thousand people, he collapsed and died on stage.

The curtain was rung down, and the theater manager addressed the audience in a very sorrowful tone: "Ladies and gentlemen, I am very sorry to inform you that Mr. Schwartzman has taken ill and is no longer with us."

From one of the last rows in the balcony, a coarse woman's voice echoed throughout the theater. "Give him an enema!" There was a hush in which a falling feather could have been heard.

"Madam," the manager said icily, looking up to the balcony, "nothing will help."

"It can't hurt!" she yelled back.

Babies Named

A new immigrant to the United States rushed his wife to the local hospital, where she was scheduled to give birth. When the nurse in attendance announced that a pair of twins had been born, a boy and a girl, the young father fainted.

When he was revived, the new father was told that his brother, the new uncle of the twins, had named the children, because there was no time to lose.

The father was very upset. "My brother is an absolute dope!" he shouted. "What does he know from names?" He paused. "All right, what did he name them?"

The nurse checked her records. "The little girl is called Denise, and the little boy, Denephew."

Commuter Time

Max Siegel was seated on the Long Island commuter train, heading home after a long, hard day at the office. A pleasant-looking young man in the adjoining seat asked for the time, but Siegel ignored him. The young man, in a louder voice, asked his neighbor for the time, and again there was no response. On a third try, the young man tapped Siegel on the shoulder and asked for the time. This time Siegel responded, giving him the time.

The young man was puzzled. "Why didn't you answer me the first time I asked you?" he said.

"Why? I'll tell you why. I give you the time, we start talking, you're a nice young man, I inquire about you, and because I have two lovely unmarried daughters at home, I invite you to come to the house for dinner. What happens? You accept, you come, my wife likes you right away, my older daughter falls in love with you, the younger one

10

approves, and suddenly it looks like you're going to be my son-in-law.

"Well, the plain truth is that I don't want to have a son-in-law who doesn't own a watch!"

Hungry Salesman

David Goldberg traveled from town to town, selling agricultural chemicals. One day he found himself in a tiny hamlet that didn't even have a diner. He was hungry, and walked into the single general store.

"Yes, sir," the owner called out.

"You sell fertilizer here?" Goldberg asked.

"We sure do," the storekeeper replied.

"Okay, so go wash your hands and make me a grilled cheese sandwich."

Subway Query

Scene: a packed New York subway car. An elderly lady turns to the woman passenger on her right. "Excuse me," she says, "you talk Jewish?" The other woman smiles and shakes her head. Undaunted, the old woman turns to her left and poses the same question to the man seated beside her. He smiles politely and shakes his head.

A straphanger standing above the old woman leans down. He says, "Excuse me, I speak Jewish. Can I help you?"

Now the old lady beams. She asks the young man standing above her, "Vot time it is, please?"

11

"Thanks, God"

An elderly Jewish visitor to Florida was hit and knocked down by a hit-and-run car. Help was summoned and within less than six minutes two ambulance attendants had transferred the old gentleman to a stretcher and had carefully ensconced him inside the ambulance. One of the ambulance attendants bent over the injured man and said:

"Are you comfortable, pop?"

The old man managed a slight smile. "Thanks, God," he said, "I make a living."

Wrong Guess

Two friends, both retired and in their senior years, were taking a walk on the Coney Island boardwalk in Brooklyn. One of them, Abe, carried an umbrella. Suddenly, the skies darkened and in a matter of moments it began to rain heavily. "Quick," his friend Solomon shouted, "open your umbrella!"

"Nah, it's no use—it's full of holes."

"So why did you take it?"

"I didn't think it would rain."

Three Names

Sol Kimelman was one of the few Jewish immigrants who came to the United States and who remained illiterate. He once learned how to sign his name in Hebrew, but that was the extent of his reading or writing ability. Nonetheless, by virtue of hard work, business sense, and luck, he became a successful businessman. He married a native-born young woman and in the course of time they were blessed with children. Each year, the Kimelman family seemed to grow more prosperous.

Whenever Sol and his wife would travel up to the Catskills for a few days of vacation, Sol would sign the register with two *X* marks. One, he understood, was for his first name, and the second for the family name.

Once, when he was nearing retirement age, and when he realized that he was quite a rich man, he began to sign his name at hotel registers with three *X*'s. A friend of his noticed and asked him why the extra *X*. And Sol said: "Well, ever since we began to have a few dollars in the bank, my wife thought it would be nicer if I also had a middle name."

Reward Offer

Abraham Greenbaum was attending a convention of his lodge in Atlantic City, long before the casinos transformed that New Jersey community. He reached into his pocket during one of the sessions, and realized his wallet was gone. Distressed, he proceeded to the dais, and got permission from the chairman to make an announcement on the public address system.

"Excuse me, ladies and gentlemen," he said, unaccustomed to the sound of his amplified voice. "I lost my wallet with eight hundred dollars. Whoever finds it, I'll give a reward of fifty dollars."

From one of the tables came an anonymous voice: "I'll give seventy-five!"

Tenth Man

A bearded man was being questioned by the judge, who was seated on his high bench, wearing the customary judicial robe.

"What do you do for a living?" the judge asked.

"I'm a *minyan* man."

"What's that?"

"In the synagogue, when they need a tenth man for services, for a minyan, you know, for a quorum, I'm the tenth man."

"That's ridiculous! If there are nine men, of course you're the tenth. I could also be the tenth man."

"Your honor, I didn't know you're Jewish."

A New Jew

Sammy Davis, Jr., the popular black entertainer, decided to convert to Judaism many years ago. In fact, he became a practicing Jew, and when he died in 1990, the funeral service was conducted by a rabbi.

Like all would-be converts, Sammy had to study the basics of Judaism and then undergo a conversion ceremony. Since he had chosen a reform rabbi, the ceremony was relatively simple and painless (among Orthodox and Conservative Jews, a male convert will generally undergo a circumcision and also a dunking rite held in a *mikva,* a special ritual bath).

At any rate, Sammy called together all of his many friends for the ceremony at which a reform rabbi would pronounce him a Jew. The rabbi spoke to the crowd of the ethical values of Judaism, and explained that since Sammy had studied and had passed the written and oral tests, he was prepared to welcome him into the Jewish community. Sammy donned a yarmulke, and with the rabbi placing his hands on the entertainer's head in a position of blessing, he announced that Sammy was now a full-fledged Jew.

People shouted *mazel tov* (congratulations), and went off to enjoy the refreshments that had been prepared. Some members of the audience noticed however that the rabbi, who enjoyed a great sense of humor, was talking privately to the famous performer.

One of the rabbi's congregants approached him and asked what he said to Sammy privately, at which point the clergyman laughed and said, "I said to him, 'Sammy, I'm happy you're now Jewish, but do me a favor—don't move into my neighborhood.' "

Dual Reasons

Jacob Wasserman lived on the Lower East Side of Manhattan in the early years of the twentieth century. A month before the High Holy Days he brought a bolt of material into a local tailor and asked that a suit be made up for him. The tailor studied the material and then measured Wasserman. "I'm sorry," he said, "I can't do it—there isn't enough material here for a suit."

Discouraged, Wasserman walked a block to another tailor and made the same request. Again the tailor examined the bolt of material, and measured Wasserman. "Okay, it'll be ready for the holidays," he said.

On the first day of Rosh Hashanah, Wasserman, clad in his new suit, went to the synagogue. To his surprise he noticed that his tailor's son, seated a few rows ahead, was wearing a suit that seemed to be made from the same material as his own new garment.

Again to his surprise the first tailor, who had turned down Wasserman's request to fashion a suit, sat down alongside him. Wasserman could not resist telling the tailor about his inadequacies.

"Look," he said, "this is my new suit. Goldfarb made it, and you said there wasn't enough material. There was even enough left over to make a suit for Goldfarb's son!"

The tailor smiled. "Yes, yes, but you see—I got twins."

Funny Fan

Scene: the Coney Island boardwalk in Brooklyn, in midsummer. The time: 1938. It's a ferociously hot day, and air conditioning is still something far off in the future. Mrs. Feigenbaum, elderly and poor, walks into a local notions store, picks up a hefty fan, gives it a swish, and asks the owner, "How much for this?"

"Two dollars—it's one of our best numbers."

She continues down the crowded aisle of the small shop until she spots a tiny paper fan, and holds it up before trying a swish. It hardly makes a ripple in the torrid air. "What kind of lousy fan is this?" she asks. "How much is it?"

"It's a nickel, but you don't wave it, lady—with this fan, you hold it up, and shake your head back and forth."

Quick Biography

It was the last train out of Penn Station for the Long Island Rail Road's commuter train to Long Beach. There were only two passengers on the train; both were adult men, in their late forties or fifties. One man seemed to be exhausted, and the other looked as though he had just gotten up from a long nap.

The tired-looking man took up a double seat, allowing him to put his legs up on the empty seat facing him. He was clearly annoyed when the second man ignored all the empty seats in the train and headed for the seat right next to him. The tired man confronted the man next to him. He said:

"Listen, my name is Fred Weinstein. I'm a lawyer, I have my own office uptown. I'm married and have three children—my son's a doctor, my older daughter is in law school, and my younger daughter is a teacher. I own my own home in Long Beach, I contribute to charity regularly, I have no hobbies, and I'm not interested in politics. Now, does that cover everything? The truth is I'm dead tired, and I've got to get some sleep in the next hour. Good night!''

Suicidal Tip

Bernie was walking his dog one summer evening along the riverbank. Looking up, he saw one of his neighbors, Mendel, poised on the bridge, obviously about to jump into the swirling current below.

"Wait!" Bernie yelled. "Please, have a heart, don't do it, Mendel. I mean, if you want to end it, I don't care, but think of me. If you go into the river, I have to jump in after you, and I can't swim, so I'll drown, and then my wife will become a widow and my four children will become orphans, and life will be very tough for them. Do me a favor, be a good Jew, get off the bridge, get dressed, go home, and then you can go down to the basement and hang yourself!''

Next of Kin

Three friends are inveterate gin rummy players. They play on the commuter train, in each other's homes, outdoors, indoors, daytime, nighttime. Once the three men were playing in a neighborhood coffee shop; without warning, one of the friends,

Isaac Deutsch, suffered a stroke, collapsed, and died.

The two remaining friends knew that one of them had to inform the widow immediately, and finally they decided between them that Hy Kaplan would go. He got into his car, drove a few blocks to the Deutsch home, knocked on the door, and when his friend's wife appeared at the door, he said:

"Listen, Molly, Isaac lost a lot of money tonight at cards."

"He should only have a stroke!" Mrs. Deutsch snapped.

"He already had."

Hunger Pangs

During the years of the Great Depression, roughly from 1930 through 1938, it was not uncommon for Jewish families who were fortunate enough to have heated apartments to live in to toss down a few pennies, wrapped in a piece of old newspaper, to men who played a few bars on an old violin. Sometimes, these itinerants would knock on a door and ask for help directly.

One day Mrs. Greenberg opened the door to a knock. An obviously impoverished, unemployed man stood there, his head lowered.

"Please, lady," he whispered. "I didn't eat in three days already."

"You should force yourself!" she shouted at him.

Toothbrush for One

A traveling salesman named Bloom, en route to Milwaukee, lost his suitcase. At the station rest-room he turned to a man using the adjoining sink and asked if he could borrow some soap, and the stranger readily agreed. A few minutes later Bloom explained that he had lost his baggage, and could he borrow some shaving cream and a razor—and again the stranger using the adjoining sink readily agreed.

Now, washed up and freshly shaved, Bloom turned again to the stranger. "Mind if I borrow your toothbrush?" he asked. This time, the stranger balked, and looked at Bloom as though he were not quite all there. "Why don't you buy one at the drugstore?" the man said to Bloom, who responded, "Anti-Semite!"

Japanese Convert

Tom Hasakawee was a very rare individual. Of Japanese ancestry, he had converted to Judaism when he was still a teenager, and somehow had landed a job with a tiny synagogue in a small town in Indiana. He was a combination beadle-Hebrew teacher, cantor-kosher meat purveyor-mohel. On occasion, when the rabbi was away or ill, Tom could deliver an interesting sermon. He had been with the same congregation for more than forty years.

One day the synagogue's *bale'batim*, the movers and shakers of the synagogue, called him in and announced that he was being let go. Tom was dumbfounded.

"Why?" he asked. "Don't you like the way I take care of the synagogue and teach the children their lessons? Don't you like the way I sing at the services? The meat I provide is not tasty and healthful? Why?"

Judge Horowitz, the synagogue's president, cleared his throat. "No, no, Tom, it's none of that. Everyone loves you and respects you—you do a great job. It's just that—lately, we've been getting complaints from the younger members. When you perform a *bris,* a circumcision, it's the way you raise the scalpel and scream *HEI!* It scares the hell out of them."

Rejected Suitor

A young man in a suburban town outside Chicago approaches the owner of a chain of stores, a highly successful businessman.

"Mr. Levy," the bearded young man says, "I have come here to ask for your daughter's hand in matrimony."

Levy slowly puts the cigar he had been smoking into the ashtray on his large desk.

"Listen, you punk," he replies, his voice deliberately low. "You don't work, you don't go to school, you sponge off your folks, I don't like the way you speak or the way you dress or the way your hair reaches down to your *pupik* (navel). I don't like a single thing about you. In fact, pick yourself up and walk out of here, right now, before

I'm tempted to call security and have you thrown out into the gutter, where you belong."

The young man rose, walked to the door, turned the knob, and then turned back to Levy.

"So I guess the answer is no, right?"

Future Plans

Overheard in a Jewish nursing home in Los Angeles:

Two ladies of advanced years are reminiscing and philosophizing. Says one:

"You know, I can understand it when a young woman marries an older man, a rabbi—she becomes a *rebbetsin,* a very honored position. Or when a young woman marries an older man, a doctor—she becomes a *doctorshe,* also a respectable position. But when a young woman marries a rich old widower, what's the point?"

"Silly! She wants to become a rich widow. It's not so bad."

And the Hat?

Grandmother Belsky took her grandson to the beach in Westhampton. She was staying with her son's family, and the afternoon was hers, to enjoy the company of her three-year-old grandson Matthew, named for her late husband, Mendel. The small boy was wearing a summerweight sailor suit, complete with a ribboned cap.

Mrs. Belsky closed her eyes, she remembered,

for only a moment; when she awoke from the light nap, she looked around for her grandson, became hysterical when she couldn't find him, and then saw the huge waves that were now battering the shore. The child had been swept out to sea! He was nowhere to be seen, and there was no one to help. She turned her face heavenward and began to cry and pray, all at once:

"Oh, dear Lord, maybe I'm not the most religious woman in the world, but I promise, I swear, return my grandson to me safe and sound, and I will go to synagogue regularly, I will be meticulous about the laws of kosher food, please God—" And then, miraculously, she saw the child borne on a wave that landed him on the shore, almost at her feet. She rushed over to the boy, who was wet and crying, but otherwise seemed to be all right.

Mrs. Belsky turned her eyes skyward again. "Thank you, dear Lord," she said. "Thank you. But—where's his hat?"

Miami Voices

Two old friends are relaxing in Miami's sun. They're in their swimsuits, sprawled in lounge chairs, looking at the paper, and listening to a transistor radio.

"Morris, we've been friends a long, long time, so I want to ask you a personal question—you still have interest in making love?" Al asks.

"Well, Al, I'll tell you . . ."

"Come on, Morris—how often? Every week?"

"No."

"Every month?"

"Eh, no, no."

"Once a year, every winter?"

"Al, look at us, we're sitting in the sun in Florida. It's warm. This you call a winter?"

"Much Prettier"

Adele Feinberg always felt she had a good life. Her husband was exemplary, and when she learned he had a mistress she decided to look away. Maybe that's the way things are done nowadays, she rationalized.

One day the Feinbergs went to the opera. They had choice seats overlooking the orchestra. At one point, before the performance began, an attractive young woman looked up at them and smiled warmly.

"Who's that?" Mrs. Feinberg asked.

Her husband hesitated for only a moment, and then whispered, "You know, my mistress."

"And who's the red-haired woman with her?"

"Oh, that's Greenstone's mistress."

Mrs. Feinberg smiled happily. She turned to her husband. "You know," she said, "ours is much prettier."

Bovine Bliss

For decades Jewish families in the Northeast have been spending their summer vacations in the Catskills, a beautiful resort and farming area located about one hundred miles north of New York City. Many of the vacationers relaxed in the hotels that dotted the region, while others took cabins for the whole summer and established what amounted to a family summer camp ambience for eight or ten weeks every year. Since these bungalows had kitchens where the tenants could prepare their own meals, they came to be known as *coch-a'lains*— cook-yourself places. Some families went to the same bungalow colonies for years, and formed long-term friendships.

Here and there were farms owned and run by Jewish families, some of whom had been in the area for two or three generations. One such farm was owned by a recently widowed farmer named Jake Gottlieb. He was now in the second year of his widowhood, and since he was in his early forties, he had it in mind to marry a second time. But like many farmers, Jake was a very cautious man. He had met the daughter of one of the summer bungalow families, a schoolteacher in her early thirties, who he thought would make a good wife, and who he believed was interested in him. They had taken long walks together, dined out a number of times, and had even gone dancing in the local posh hotel ballrooms. But Jake wanted to be sure that if he married Miriam, the teacher, they would have a good sex life together. She had never permitted him to go beyond a good-night kiss.

One afternoon he invited her to his farm, and proudly showed her around. They walked for a while to the pasture and came across a bull who had just mounted a cow and was doing what bulls and cows do in such circumstances.

25

Jake turned to Miriam, a twinkle in his eye. "That looks like fun," he said.

Smiling, Miriam responded, "So, who's stopping you? I'm sure the cow wouldn't mind."

Change the Order

Jacob Wasserman had worked as a clothing manufacturer on Seventh Avenue in New York for more than forty years. When he was sixty-five he decided to retire and to give himself a great big farewell party. He arranged for a caterer to bring into his office the choicest morsels, a bar was set up, and hundreds of Jacob's customers, employees, friends, and relatives were invited. People ate and drank, everyone wished him well, some people brought gifts, and then the party was over, and Jacob, a bachelor, found himself alone.

He felt cheated somehow by the lack of genuine joy in his autumn years. He called in his messenger and asked him to bring him a beautiful, sexy young woman who would spend the night with him, and also to get him some cocaine and marijuana.

An hour later the messenger phoned: "Mr. Wasserman, I got the drugs you wanted, but I just can't seem to find the kind of young lady you're looking for. What should I do?"

Wasserman pondered. "Listen, just cancel the order. Instead, bring me a Danish and coffee."

26

Wrong Bus

Stories of immigrant Jewish families that came to the United States with almost nothing and succeeded beyond their wildest dreams in the "Golden Land" are legion. Many of the newcomers became major donors to various charitable and cultural enterprises, while others preferred to display their newfound wealth ostentatiously.

The story is told, for example, of one couple that started out life in America in a cold-water flat on the Lower East Side of New York, and who managed, by dint of hard work, much luck, good business sense, and meeting knowledgeable people who advised them well in matters of investment, to become very affluent.

They were now in their late sixties, new tenants in an expensive and very desirable Park Avenue apartment, retired from business, and anxious to move up in the world and mingle with cultured Americans, hoping no doubt that some of the culture would rub off on them. The couple, whose names were Anna and Joseph Rabinowitz, had never really graduated from high school, and try as they might, they still retained a strong trace of a Polish-Yiddish accent.

One evening they were excited by the prospect of a musicale to which they had been invited. The party was slated to be held in the penthouse of a Central Park West apartment building, and Mr. Rabinowitz was giving his wife some last-minute instructions as they waited for the limousine they had hired for the evening to take them to the musicale, at which funds would be raised for a new orchestral group.

"Just listen to me, Anna," her husband said, his tone forceful and commanding. "I want you not to say a word; keep your mouth closed. These people we'll be with, they're very educated, very high class. Let them do the talking, you listen and try to learn something." His wife, who enjoyed conversing with people, nodded in agreement. She knew that both she and her husband were culturally inferior to almost every person at the soiree, but hoped that her appearance and bearing would help cover up her lack of education.

They were now at the party, sipping drinks, munching on hors d'oeuvres, listening to the talk that swirled around them, smiling, and trying to enjoy themselves. Earlier in the evening when the host had appealed for funds for the orchestra, the Rabinowitz couple had gotten warm applause when they presented the host with a $1,000 check.

They were seated now, listening intently to a conversation between two obviously educated men, one of whom sported a goatee. The bearded one had just announced that "no one can come close to Mozart, no one—he's beyond reach— people can't even see him!" At which point, Mrs. Rabinowitz, totally unable to control herself, having been wordless for more than two hours, suddenly popped up:

"What are you talking?" she interjected. "I saw Mozart on the Number Five bus that goes to Brooklyn only last week."

The conversation stopped cold. Nobody said a word, and no one looked at anyone else, especially not at Mrs. Rabinowitz or her spouse. After a while, the conversation continued, as though Mozart had never existed or been mentioned.

When the Rabinowitz couple were in their limousine being driven back to their apartment, the husband turned on his wife, his expression angry and his voice low and furious. "You stupid thing, you," he said. "You had to open your big mouth and show everyone how backward you are. Everybody knows the Number Five bus don't go to Brooklyn!"

Shakespeare Plus

In the 1920s and 1930s, New York's Second Avenue, adjoining the teeming and always crowded Lower East Side, was virtually the Broadway of Yiddish Theater. A dozen or so full-fledged theaters seating perhaps a total of 15,000 to 20,000 people every evening offered a wide variety of dramas, musicals, comedies, and even tragedies. Many of the shows were devoted to Jewish themes, and many were more universal in approach.

This was long before the advent of television, and even before every family in the country enjoyed the movies. Some of the plays that were produced were Yiddish translations of the classics, including Ibsen, Molière, and Shakespeare. Out of this Yiddish background came some of America's leading actors, including the late Paul Muni and Edward G. Robinson.

One of the great stars of the Yiddish stage was an actor and manager by the name of Maurice

Schwartz. He was an imposing personality, who directed and starred in numerous performances. He was also far from shy. He personally took a hand in helping to translate Shakespeare. Thus, there appeared one season a marquee that proclaimed (in Yiddish) KING LEAR by WILLIAM SHAKESPEARE. FARTEITCHT UN FARBES-ERT FUN MAURICE SCHWARTZ (translated and improved by Maurice Schwartz).

Why So Many?

Isaac Shneider came to the United States on a visit during the 1930s, before the outbreak of World War II and after the worst of the Depression years. He was a reasonably successful professor in his native Poland, and as an academic was always in search of knowledge and understanding. He was greeted in New York by his cousin, Fred Fink, who in the old country had been known as Feibish Finkelstein.

After touring the main tourist sights in New York, Isaac was seated in his cousin's apartment in Brooklyn. Somewhat pedantically he asked his American cousin:

"How many people are there in New York?"

"Eight million."

"And how many Jews are there in New York?"

"About two million."

Isaac merely nodded his head and mumbled something that sounded like hm, hm, hm.

The next day Isaac took the train to visit another relative who lived in Cincinnati. Again he was taken on a tour of the usual tourist sites, and again he questioned his cousin:

"How many people are there in Cincinnati?"

"About a million."

"And how many Jews are there?"

"Oh, not many, about fifty thousand."

And again Isaac nodded his head, and seemed to mumble to himself. When he returned to New York and prepared to embark for the return trip to Europe, his cousin asked him for his reaction to his trip.

"It's a beautiful, wonderful country," Isaac replied. "But how come there are so many Gentiles?"

Glass of Tea

Sam Lieberman was what is known as a "paintner"—a housepainter, who gets the extra *n* to distinguish him from an artist.

Sam was in his early seventies and thinking of retirement, and only took on new jobs occasionally. He had just completely repainted an Upper East Side apartment—it had taken him four days—and was a little annoyed to get a phone call from the lady of the house.

Unbeknownst to Sam, the woman's husband had accidentally smeared the wet wall in the bedroom the night before. When Sam came to the apartment, the mistress of the house said:

"Oh, I'm so glad you came over. Come into the bedroom with me, I want to show you where my husband put his hand last night."

Sam stared at her. "Listen, lady," he said. "I'm

31

not so young anymore. Just give me a glass of tea
with lemon. That I'll appreciate.''

Yankee in the South

Moishe Tenenbaum was a Hassid who almost never
left his Brooklyn neighborhood, where nearly all
the other men looked like him and dressed like him.
For this particular group of Hassidic Jews, the long
black caftan, long white hose, a fur-trimmed round
black hat, and of course the uncut sidecurls were
standard.

One day Moishe's rabbi, a saintly man who ran
a chain of small yeshivas—religious schools—in
Brooklyn, called him and asked if he would mind
traveling to a small town in Alabama for a few days.
The rabbi explained that he had heard from a
wealthy man in that community who wished to
make a substantial donation to the yeshivas, but
preferred to hand the check over to a real, live,
genuine Hassid. Moishe agreed, and soon was on
a bus heading south. The trip was long and tiring,
and after three days of almost continuous travel,
Moishe arrived in the Alabama community. The
bus deposited him in the middle of town, where the
bus depot was located.

Within minutes, Moishe was surrounded by a
group of curious men and boys, many of whom
seemed to be loitering in the area. The townspeople
stared hard at Moishe, never before having seen
anyone dressed quite like him, and certainly none

of them having ever seen a man with long, uncut sidecurls. They did not look threatening, but Moishe—tired, dirty, and hungry from his long trip—was annoyed by their rude stares.

Finally he blurted out: "What's the matter? Ain'tcha never seen a Yankee before?"

Former Employees?

Morris Feingold is desperate for a job, and after many weeks of unemployment he is seated at the desk of the personnel director of a major publishing company, known for its American history encyclopedias and reference books. The personnel man looks dubious as he glances over the employment application in front of him.

"You say you have a great deal of experience selling books door to door," the interviewer says.

"Yes sir, years and years of experience."

"And it says here you earned a master's degree in American history from Yale University."

"Yes sir, that's right."

The personnel director nods. "All right, I'll recommend that you be hired," he says, rising from his desk. "Wait here a minute, I want to get some forms for you to sign."

Morris looks around the office, and for the first time notices portraits of Washington and Lincoln on the wall behind him. "Nice-looking men," he comments, pointing to the pictures. "Were they with the company also?"

"Not Fair"

During the tough Depression years of the 1930s, life in America was very difficult for everyone. Because they were newcomers, recently arrived immigrants found it perhaps a little harder than most, because essentially they did not understand what was going on around them—to them a crash meant when the piano came tumbling down the stairs. Try as they might, they could not fathom the concept of a stock-market crash.

Many of the immigrant Jewish families tried to protect themselves through the purchase of life insurance policies, and it was a common scene to see a life insurance salesman going from home to home, collecting twenty-five or fifty cents toward the premium, which gave people the feeling that at least there was some protection to look forward to, if disaster struck.

One evening Mr. Goldstein was explaining to his wife about the new life insurance policy he had bought. "If I die in an accident," he said, "you'll get ten thousand dollars, but if I die naturally, from sickness or old age, then you only get five thousand. They call it a double indemnity."

It took a while for Mrs. Goldstein to absorb the information. Finally, she spoke up, her tone betraying anger: "It's not fair," she said. "If, God forbid, you die a natural death, then I only get half!"

"Too Busy"

Sam Levine came to the United States as a small child, and grew up in a poor home. He studied hard in school, worked hard at the small business he established, and sure enough, by the time he was in his early sixties and ready to retire, he had become a very rich man.

He was not a social climber and maintained his lifelong friendships with the same people with whom he had grown up. One day he decided that he needed a new, large painting to adorn a large wall in a fancy apartment he had rented in New York. At his friends' suggestion he commissioned an artist who was known for his nonrepresentational style.

After six months Sam invited his friends to a party at his home at which the new artwork would be unveiled. Everyone, the artist and the guests, looked forward to Sam's reaction to the large canvas, knowing that it had cost him $50,000. At last the moment of truth arrived—the artist, standing alongside Sam, and surrounded by dozens of friends, uncovered his work. And there, on an immense easel, was a huge, blank canvas, featuring one splotch of orange in the middle. No one said a word, waiting for Sam's verdict.

"I like it," Sam said. "Very nice." Everyone breathed a sigh of relief.

One year later: same apartment, same artist, same guests, and of course the host, Sam Levine, who, everyone knew, had commissioned a second painting for another blank wall. Again, the painting was unveiled and again everyone waited for Sam's reaction. The new work was almost the same as the old one—a big, blank canvas, a splotch of orange in the middle, only now there was in addition a small green dot in the lower left-hand corner.

"Well, I like it," Sam said, not wishing to offend the painter, "but it's just a little *ongue'patch'ket* (too busy)."

Wrong Number

Shirley Rosenbaum is young, married, and tries to take care of her small child while keeping up with her studies at the local college. She always seems to feel harassed, overworked, and on the verge of a nervous breakdown.

One particularly difficult morning she phones her mother. "Ma, listen, I hate to impose," she says. "Jonathan has the flu, the baby is acting funny all night, the heat is not coming up, the dishwasher broke down, and a bunch of ladies from the sister-hood are coming over for tea. I don't know what to do!"

"Take it easy, take it easy. I'm getting dressed right away, I'm taking the subway to the railroad, then I'll take the train to your town, I'll get a taxi, and I'll be at your side just as soon as possible. And don't worry about Ian, he'll be fine."

"Ian? Who's Ian?"

"What do you mean? Ian is your baby boy."

"No, no, my baby's name is Jeremy. Wait a minute—is this 677-4109?"

"No, this is 677-4190."

Shirley lets the information sink in; her voice is now reduced to a whisper. "So, does this mean you're not coming?"

2

Meanwhile, Back in Israel

Alan King, the comedian and theatrical producer, was once asked why he is so devoted to Israel. After all, his questioner noted, he is an American, born and bred in Brooklyn. "Yes," he explained, with a twinkle. "America is my wife, and I love her deeply—but Israel is my mother, and I love her too!"

Although Israel is only as small as New Jersey (not counting the still unresolved issue of the West Bank and Gaza Strip), and is now only in the fifth decade of its existence, it holds a very deep and important spot in the hearts of the Jewish people, no matter where they live.

For nearly two thousand years, the wandering Jews have survived with one hope on their lips—Zion. "We will yet return to Israel and be again as we were, in days of yore," they prayed. And now that it has actually happened, many Jews still rub their eyes, not quite believing that the dream of two millennia has been realized. They look in wonderment, they marvel, they support, and they laugh—not quite sure how to react to this historical phenomenon.

Ready, Aim, Fire!

In 1973 Egypt and Syria attacked Israel on Yom Kippur, the holiest day of the Jewish year. Thousands of reservists rushed to their assigned posts directly from attending synagogue services; some of the men never even removed their prayer shawls.

One of the lesser-known battles took place at sea, where an Israeli submarine, captained by a member of the Rothschild family, found itself a few hundred yards from an Egyptian destroyer, protected by heavy fog. Captain Rothschild ordered the immediate descent of his vessel, and told the torpedo man to ready his deadly weapon. Israel was about to sink an enemy destroyer that was not more than five hundred yards away.

The submarine worked itself into position, the crewmembers were excited, the torpedo room was at full battle station, and Yosef the torpedo man had his finger on the red button that would send the lethal weapon into the side of the enemy warship.

Everyone's heart was pounding as preparations for the attack continued. When anyone spoke, it was in a whisper. Yosef turned to his captain, the scion of the illustrious billionaire family. "Captain," he whispered, "how much does a torpedo

40

cost?'' The captain looked at his torpedo man strangely. ''Cost? Who cares? Just get ready!''

''Captain, how much?'' Yosef persisted. Impatiently Rothschild shot back, ''Twenty-five thousand dollars—now wait for my signal.''

In thirty seconds the Israeli captain turned to Yosef and commanded, ''Fire!'' Nothing happened. Yosef kept his finger on the red button, but did not press it. ''Fire!'' Rothschild shouted. ''Fire!'' Yosef did not budge.

Now visually exasperated, Rothschild yelled at his torpedo man, ''All right! All right! I'll pay for it myself.'' At which point the torpedo was released and within moments found its mark in the Egyptian destroyer.

K Rations in Israel

A young Israeli who had fought in the Six Day War came to the United States for a well-deserved rest and vacation. He was in the regular army of the Jewish State, and was surprised to learn, when he met a distant cousin in Philadelphia, that the latter was also a full-time soldier in the U.S. army. They talked and compared notes and found there were many gripes common to both the American and the Israeli troops.

''Well, there's one thing you don't have in Israel,'' the American sergeant said to his Israeli cousin, ''and that's K rations. I hate them, they're terrible, but when you're hungry and there's nothing else to eat, you eat that stuff.''

The Israeli retorted, ''We have K rations also—

maybe not like yours, but that's what we call them. Listen, we have *knishes, kreplach, katchke, kasha, kugel, kishke,* and for dessert, *kichel.*"

Attack the U.S.?

Two Israeli veterans of the 1948 War of Independence are sitting at an outdoor café alongside the Tel Aviv esplanade. Shmuel, the older of the two, says to his friend Yitzhak:

"You know I think I finally figured out all our financial problems. What we should do is what the Germans and Japanese did—first they declared war on America, then they got defeated, and then America came along, rebuilt them, and now these two countries are richer and stronger than America. It's a terrific plan, it can't lose!"

Cautiously, Yitzhak examines his friend's suggestion, and then says:

"All right, I'll grant you Germany and Japan are today very strong and very rich, and that America built them up. But don't forget, they were both defeated by America. With our luck, we'll declare war against America, and we'll win! Then what'll we do?"

Right to Left

Leon Blum was once the prime minister of France. A kibbutz, Kfar Blum, is named for him. (There is also a kibbutz called Kfar Truman, for the former president of the U.S., and an imposing memorial

42

known as the Kennedy Memorial Forest.) Blum was a French Jew and a committed Socialist.

Once he was visiting the Jewish community in Palestine, before the establishment of Israel. Ben-Gurion and Golda Meir were showing him around. At lunch, Blum thanked his hosts and said he was very favorably impressed by everything he had seen. He added: "However, I am first a Frenchman, and then a Socialist, and finally a Jew."

Ben-Gurion quipped: "Yes, but here in the Land of Israel, we read and write from right to left."

He Didn't Ask

A tourist in Haifa had lost his way in the rented car he had taken out the day before. With its meandering streets and various levels that remind visitors of San Francisco, Haifa is an easy city to get lost in. This particular tourist spotted what looked like a parking space, but he wasn't entirely sure it was permissible to stop there. A policeman was standing nearby, and the visitor stuck his head out of the window, getting the policeman's attention.

"Shalom!" the tourist said. "Can I park there?" he asked, pointing to the questionable space, where another car was already ensconced.

"Absolutely not," the policeman said.

"So why is that car parked there?" the visitor asked.

The policeman shrugged, a slight smile beginning to appear on his face. "He didn't ask me," he said.

Clean Dishes in Sudan

An Israeli businessman, Z'ev Sharet, was traveling through Africa seeking customers for his plant's products, and investigating import possibilities at the same time. After several weeks of travel, mostly by air, he was now on a KLM flight from Nairobi, Kenya, to Cyprus, where he planned to catch an airliner for the short hop to Tel Aviv.

As the jumbo Boeing 747 sped across Sudan northward, the pilot announced on the public address system that because of a minor problem in one of the four powerful engines that propelled the aircraft, they would make an unexpected stopover in Khartoum.

"We should be on the ground about an hour, that's all," the pilot said. The Israeli, however, became panicky. He carried an Israeli passport, he was probably the only Jewish passenger on board, Sudan was a Moslem nation—he could be snatched away, and no one would ever be able to trace him.

Sharet spoke to the chief steward and explained his predicament. The Dutch crewmember said he would confer with the captain in the cockpit. In about ten minutes, the steward returned, beckoned Sharet into the plane's galley, and said:

"Put on this white jacket, and this cap. Now, as soon as we land, start washing dishes. There'll probably be a few soldiers coming on board; just ignore them, you wash dishes. If none of the other passengers says anything, it'll be all right."

Sharet nodded, struggled into the white jacket, which was too tight, donned the cap, which was too big, and began washing dishes. He washed them again and again, and did not stop until after the captain announced they were taking off for Cyprus. When the Israeli returned to his seat, the steward handed him a glass and a bottle of cognac.

"You earned this," he said. "Our dishes have never been cleaner."

More Postage

An American tourist in Israel enters the post office and asks a clerk if the postage he has affixed to the letter is enough for air mail to the U.S. The clerk weighs the letter and says, "No, you'll have to add an additional shekel's worth of stamps. It's too heavy."

The tourist retrieves the letter, ponders, and then says to the postal clerk: "And if I add another shekel's worth of postage, it'll become lighter? Huh!"

How to "Decamel"

A Chicago tourist visits ancient Beersheba, known as the gateway to Israel's vast Negev desert. He notices that an enterprising Israeli has a camel on a long leash, and offers visitors a lift up on the beast and a chance to be photographed astride the tall creature.

"How much do you charge?" the Chicagoan asks.

"One shekel to go up on the camel and have a photo taken."

"And from this you make a living?"

"Not quite—I also charge five shekels to get off."

Burglary Explained

A judge sentences a burglar to a prison term. The prisoner, an elderly Jew, looks embarrassed and crestfallen. He notices a reporter making notes about the case, and calls out to him:

"Please, sir, don't write about me in the paper— I have a wife and two children at home; if they read about me, they'll be too ashamed to walk the street."

"Why didn't you think of that before you started burglarizing?"

"What do you mean why? Who do you think I did it for, heh?"

Kissinger's Suit

When Henry Kissinger was U.S. Secretary of State he once received a gift from an admirer. It consisted of a bolt of fine cloth, suitable for a man's suit. The gift giver had suggested that whenever Mr. Kissinger was in London he should take the material to a local tailor and have a custom-made suit made up for him.

Sure enough, a few weeks later Kissinger was

in London, and he brought the cloth to a reputable tailoring establishment in Oxford St. When the cloth was unfurled, however, the tailor in charge told Kissinger that he was very sorry, but there simply was not enough material to fashion a suit of clothes for him. Disappointed, Kissinger took the bolt of cloth, and during subsequent trips to Paris and Rome the local tailors told him the same thing.

A few months later Kissinger was in Tel Aviv, and he decided to try a local tailor. The gentleman in question examined the cloth, and then measured Kissinger carefully, and finally announced: "No problem, we can make a beautiful suit for you, a jacket, a pair of trousers, a vest, and it's even possible we'll have enough material left over to make you an extra pair of trousers."

Kissinger was astounded, and told the Israeli tailor about his experiences in London, Paris, and Rome. The elderly tailor nodded, and then said softly, "Well, I understand, sir, but the truth is that by us in Israel, you're not such a big man like you are in those other places."

Funny Film Hat

An Israeli woman wearing a hat crowned with several feathers and plumes had just made herself comfortable in the movie theater. She turned around to the man seated behind her, and asked if her hat disturbed him, in which case she would remove it. "No, no," he said, "it's much funnier than the film we're about to see on the screen."

A Cautious Boy

Security is always uppermost in the minds of Israelis. Yosef, a youngster of eleven, was cautioned by his parents to be careful in talking to strangers.

One afternoon he was walking his dog in the field, not far from the main highway. A car pulled up and the passenger seated alongside the driver called out:

"Tell me, kid, how far is it to Jerusalem?"

"It depends on how fast you travel," the boy replied carefully.

"What's your name, kid?"

"I have the same name my grandfather had."

"And what was your grandfather's name?"

"The same as his grandfather's—our family names its children for the grandfather."

"Are there any more kids like you at home?"

"As many as my mother sets the table for."

"And how many settings would that be?"

"In our house, every person has his own setting."

"Stop Praying!"

A Yemenite Jew who already had seven children at home brought his pregnant wife to the hospital. The doctor told him that the birth would be complicated, so the Yemenite brought along his brothers and sisters, all of whom sat outside the hospital reciting Psalms for the pregnant woman. After a few hours the young husband-father entered the hospital; when he saw that his wife was not in her room, he asked the nurse on duty what the situation was. She replied:

"Well, one baby, a boy, has already arrived. But there are more coming."

At which point the Yemenite rushed out to his family, all of whom were still reciting Psalms, and shouted, "Stop, for God's sake, please, stop praying!"

Fixing Shoes

A new immigrant in Israel wanted to have a pair of shoes resoled. She stopped a passerby and in broken Hebrew asked for "Jochanan the Cobbler Street" so she could have her shoes repaired. The Israeli said:

"Madam, on Jochanan the Cobbler Street you won't find a shoe-repair shop. Go to Allenby Street, off Nachlat Benjamin Street, and you'll see a shop."

The new immigrant seemed upset. Slowly, in imperfect Hebrew she admonished the Tel Avivian: "You are making fun of me—that's not right. I'm sure there is a shoe-repair shop on Jochanan the Cobbler Street, and not on Allenby—I know this is a street named for a famous English general. You think I'm so stupid to believe that on such a street a man will sit and fix shoes?"

Beggar's Route

Two beggars knock on the door of an apartment in Netanya. The woman of the house opens the door. She recognizes one beggar and asks why he is now coming around with a partner.

"I sold this route to my friend here," the beggar says. "I'm just introducing him to my regular customers."

Early Boycott

Two Israelis are seated in the park in Jerusalem. One sighs deeply and says he wished the Arab boycott had begun a long time ago, rather than after the establishment of Israel.

"What are you talking about?" his friend demands.

"I'll explain: if the Arabs had launched their boycott a few thousand years ago, then the Ishmaelites would not have purchased Joseph from his brethren, we Israelites would not have wound up in Egypt, we wouldn't have had to journey from Egypt to the Promised Land, we wouldn't have been exiled from our homeland by the Romans, and now, in our later years, we wouldn't have had to come back to Israel and start everything anew!"

Horses in Rear?

An American tourist who knew less than a dozen

words in Hebrew landed at Ben-Gurion Airport outside Tel Aviv, went through customs, and found a taxi. He made himself comfortable in the rear seat, after seeing his bags stowed safely in the trunk.

When the driver had taken his place, the American said:

"*Balegolah,* take me to the Hilton in Tel Aviv."

The driver did not turn on the ignition. He turned around to his passenger and asked, "What did you call me?"

"I said *balegolah*—that means driver, doesn't it?"

The cabbie thought for a moment, and then smiled. He said:

"It's an old-fashioned word. Nowadays we say *nahag* for driver—you see, a *balegolah* was the word that was used when the horses were in front—but now, well, we say *nahag.*"

Real Challenge

There was an outbreak of flu in Israel; everyone, it seemed, caught it. Mordecai, who ran a barbershop in the Rehavia section of Jerusalem for nearly forty years, went to the doctor, sure he too had caught the flu.

The doctor examined him thoroughly and then pronounced his verdict: "Mordecai, I am happy to say you don't have the flu! No, sir," he added, laughing, "you have angina."

"Angina? So why are you so happy, doctor?"

"Because I'm tired of the same flu symptoms

and remedies, that's why. Now angina, that's a real challenge!''

Defining "Conference"

A small Israeli child asks his father, a member of the Israeli diplomatic corps, "*Abba,* Papa, what is a conference?"

"A conference is a meeting where people get together, talk about important things, and then decide—to hold another conference."

"Charge!" Won War

Levi Eshkol was prime minister of Israel at the time of the Six Day War in 1967, during which Israel defeated the combined armies of Egypt, Syria, and Jordan in a masterful campaign. A few days after the euphoria of the unexpected victory had abated somewhat, Eshkol was asked by a visiting American newspaperman how little Israel had managed to defeat the Arab armies.

Eshkol laughed. "It was easy," he said. "You see, when things looked very bleak, when Egypt sent its tanks and army to our border, and then closed off our outlet to the sea at Eilat, we called up the reserves—first, we called the doctors, then the dentists, then the lawyers, and finally the accountants. We waited patiently for the right moment, and then when Moshe Dayan, our minister of defense, decided it was the right moment, and he ordered the entire Israeli army to *charge*—oh, boy, oh, boy, they know how to charge, and they charged!"

Hebraic Juice

A young American-Jewish couple traveled to Jerusalem for their honeymoon. The young husband, who had studied Hebrew in his youth, tried to impress his new wife with his mastery of the language.

One day they were walking in the Ben Yehuda Mall when they spotted a vendor selling freshly squeezed carrot juice. It was a warm day, and both the young husband and his bride wanted some. Acting as though Hebrew was second nature to him, the young man said to the vendor:

"B'vakasha, meets guever."

The vendor smiled, pushed the carrots into his juicing machine, handed the carrot juice to the young couple, and then gently corrected the husband: *"Meets guezer."*

"And what did I say?" the newlywed husband asked, switching now to English.

"Sir, you asked for a man's juice."

Tel Aviv Bar

A Jewish visitor from the United States is walking through Tel Aviv's streets when he spots a new, modern-looking bar. The idea of a bar in Israel's main commercial city intrigues him, and he steps inside. The air-conditioning is working, the place looks spotless, although, he notices, it is also deserted, except for the bartender. He takes a seat at the bar and orders a Maccabee beer.

Sipping his beer, the tourist strikes up a conversation with the bartender. He compliments the bartender on the appearance of the place, says the beer is first-rate (and orders another), and then asks:

"But tell me, how can you make a living here? I'm sitting here with you more than a half hour, and nobody has walked in."

"Don't worry, I make a nice living—from one *shikker*."

The tourist is amazed. He knows the word *shikker* means a drunk. He asks: "How can that be? How much can the poor fellow drink a month for you to make a living here?"

The Israeli smiles. "My friend, listen. You don't have to worry about me. You see, I have a very rich brother in America, and every month he *shiks*—sends—me a nice check. He's my *shikker*!"

Turkish Guests

An Israeli couple from Zichron Yaakov went abroad on a long-overdue trip around the world. After they returned home they invited their friends and neighbors to see their photos, examine their souvenirs, and hear about their travels.

"We were everywhere," reported Mrs. Zahavi. "We were in London, Paris, Geneva, Rome, we visited all the museums, and the art galleries, and the famous sites."

54

"Did you get to Turkey?" piped up a neighbor.

"Of course, we spent nearly a week in Istanbul."

"And did you see the Dardanelles?"

"Certainly—they stayed at the same hotel that we did."

Money Transfer

A young Israeli arrives in Paris for his first trip. He proceeds to a particular bordello and asks the madam in charge for a particular young lady by the name of Jacqueline. She is not available, he is told, but when he says he'll pay five hundred dollars, she is brought to him. The two proceed to a private room, where the young Israeli tells Jacqueline that he is from Israel. She smiles and tells him that she too is an Israeli. After they spend the night together, he hands her five hundred dollars.

He is back the next night, and again spends the night with the same young woman, and again hands her five hundred dollars. On the third night he returns, spends the night again with Jacqueline, and hands her the five hundred dollars.

"By the way," he says, as he prepares to leave, "regards from your grandmother."

"You know my grandmother!" Jacqueline exclaims in surprise.

"Yes. She lives in the same building that I do, in Haifa. And when she heard I was going to visit Paris, she asked me to bring you a present—fifteen hundred dollars."

Who's a Guest?

An American tourist staying at a Haifa hotel approaches the reception desk.

"Can I have an envelope?" he asks the clerk.

"Are you a guest here?" the young clerk asks.

"A guest? I'm paying seventy-five dollars a day, so you can't call me a guest!"

Identifying the Pope

During Israel's early years, the Pope paid a visit to the Galilee area and was photographed talking with a high Israeli official. When the photo was published in the Israeli papers, two friends were talking about the event and the picture in the paper. "Which one is the Pope?" asked one of the Israelis. "He's the one with the yarmulke," said the other.

Chinese Visitors

Scene: A Jerusalem nightclub. The place is packed, with ninety percent of the customers Chinese tourists on a package tour from Hong Kong. They are mostly young people, in their twenties and thirties. The MC tries to get some of them to come up to the mike and entertain, but they seem to be shy. Finally he calls out, "Do you know any Hebrew songs? Israeli songs?" There is a dead silence until the MC adds, "Do you know 'Hava Nagila'?" Suddenly, the place explodes; everyone knows this popular number. The band joins in; everyone—

Chinese, Israelis, and even, one likes to believe, some of the Arab waiters—joins in, as the words and tune of this universal song waft over Jerusalem.

The MC calls out: "How do you happen to know 'Hava Nagila'?"

And 300 Chinese tourists call out together, "Harry Belafonte!"

What's in a Name?

In a Tel Aviv courtroom, a policeman is called on to testify in an auto accident case. The young lawyer hopes no one notices that this is the first time he is entirely on his own in court.

"What is your name?" he asks the police officer.

"Eli Cohen."

"Don't give me that! In this country there are thousands of Cohens—give me your real name."

"William Shakespeare."

"That's more like it."

Taxpayer Pays

An Israeli paper ran a contest among its readers, who were asked to respond to the line, "How do I serve society?"

An actor wrote: I entertain everyone.

A policeman wrote: I protect everybody.

A rabbi wrote: I pray for everybody.

A doctor wrote: I heal everyone.

And an ordinary taxpayer wrote: I pay for everybody.

Unknown Author

An American tourist in Tel Aviv was about to enter the impressive Mann Auditorium to take in a concert by the Israel Philharmonic. He was admiring the unique architecture, the sweeping lines of the entrance, and the modern decor throughout the building. Finally he turned to his escort and asked if the building was named for Thomas Mann, the world-famous author.

"No," his friend said, "it's named for Fredric Mann, from Philadelphia."

"Really? I never heard of him. What did he write?"

"A check."

No Time to Change

David Ben-Gurion hated to wear anything but a pair of old pants and an open, short-sleeved white shirt, without a tie of course. One day, in the early years of Israel, he had to attend a formal diplomatic function at a posh Tel Aviv hotel. Reluctantly he allowed himself to get dressed up in a full-dress Prince Albert outfit, top hat, gloves, tiepin, the works.

He remained at the diplomatic celebration for as long as was necessary, and as soon as possible he rushed away to a convention of Mapai, the Israeli workers' party. All the men in the audience were dressed in open shirts, old slacks, and some men even wore shorts, since Israel's summers can get pretty hot.

Ben-Gurion arrived late for the convention and was escorted at once up to the dais. Moments later he was introduced and he grabbed the microphone. "*Chaverim,* comrades," he called out, "I wish to apologize for my appearance, and explain that these are my working clothes—I had no time to change."

Texan in Israel

A Texan farmer is visiting Israel. He stops at a small farmhouse in the Galilee and asks for a glass of water. He is invited into the house, and the Texan and Israeli talk about their respective farms.

"How much acreage do you have here?" the American asks.

"Well, on one side, in the front, about two acres, and in the rear, about four acres."

The Texan, asked about his own farm, says he has breakfast early in the morning, gets into his car, steps on the gas, and drives and drives until sundown. "And even then I don't reach the end of my farm," he explains.

The Israeli is sympathetic. "You know, I once had a car like that also."

How to Make a Million

An American-Jewish tourist is visiting Israel. There he meets an American who settled in the old-new land more than thirty years ago. The visitor is impressed by the veteran settler's home, swimming pool, car, and modern conveniences. He surmises that his host is a millionaire.

"Tell me," the American says, "how do you become a millionaire in Israel?"

"Easy—come with two million, and soon you'll have one."

Knesset Parties

England has one of the oldest parliaments in the world, in which essentially two parties are represented. Some 600 people sit in the British parliament. In Israel, the Knesset, with only 120 seats, one of the newest parliaments in the world, has some 15 parties!

◆◆◆◆◆◆◆◆◆◆◆ **3** ◆◆◆◆◆◆◆◆◆◆◆

Jews in a Gentile World

Although the world's Jewish population in the 1990s stands at around thirteen million, sometimes it seems that half the world is Jewish. So many creative people—in the arts, sciences, education— are Jewish, but the hard facts are very different. The Jewish people is numerically tiny (in the United States, Jews are less than three percent of the population), and this reality often colors Jews' perceptions of themselves; i.e., consciously or otherwise, they know they are a minuscule group in a vast, Gentile world. This realization of course helps to explain the feeling of familial closeness that most Jews have for one another, even total strangers, when they meet in strange, foreign places.

A Church Painter

In Tel Aviv, a church was being repainted. Shlomo Feldman, who had been a housepainter for nearly

61

thirty years, was high up on a ladder, rolling paint along the building's ceiling. Suddenly, he lost his footing, the ladder began to wobble, and the hapless Israeli fell nearly fifty feet. Of all places, he landed in a baptismal font, and was knocked out.

At that point a priest passed by. He tried to rouse the painter but couldn't. He made the sign of the cross over him, uttered a few Latin phrases, and was about to leave, when Feldman awoke.

"What happened? Where am I?" he asked.

"You're in the church in Tel Aviv, I found you in the font, and I just bestowed a blessing on you— you're now a Christian," the priest said.

"Christian? What are you saying? I'm a Jew, my father's a Jew, my mother's a Jew, I don't know what you're talking about."

"You were a Jew; now you're a Christian," the young cleric said. "I should know, I've done these conversions many times. I have to go now. Good luck!"

Feldman went home, still feeling a little shaky after his fall. He called out to his wife, "Rachel, you want to hear what happened to me today at work?" From the kitchen she shot back, "No time, I'm late for my tennis game. Supper's on the table." The painter knocked on his daughter's door. "Miriam," he called out, "you want to hear what happened to me today at work?" The door was thrown open, and his daughter, a striking young lady of nineteen, came dashing out. "No time, *abba*. I can hear Dani honking his horn downstairs. Bye!" Miffed, Feldman walked down the hall of the airy apartment and knocked on the door of his seventeen-year-old son, Gavriel. Before he could even ask his question, the painter saw his son speed by, clutching a basketball. "Hi, I'm late—the guys are anxious to get started. See you tonight!"

Feldman sat down on the living room couch, thinking over the events of the day. He thought to himself: "Look, I'm a Christian only a few hours, and already I hate three Jews."

A Substitute Check

A very affluent philanthropist who had supported many religious and educational agencies throughout his life felt that he was nearing the end. He summoned three friends, a rabbi, a minister, and a priest, who had over the years guided him in the disposition of his donations to various causes.

The dying man told the three clergymen that he had provided funds in his will for the various institutions they supported, but he also had a request of them—would each of them, as his casket was being lowered into the ground, please toss an envelope with three thousand dollars in cash into the grave with him.

"I know it may sound silly," he said in a faint voice, "but if I really am headed for another place, I may need the money." He then handed the three their respective envelopes.

He died during the night and the funeral took place shortly afterward. After the interment, the three clergymen got together and compared notes. The minister said, "You know, we desperately need a new roof—I just tossed in one thousand dollars." The priest confessed, "I did exactly the same

thing—our school expenses this year are terrible.''
The rabbi said, ''Well, I tossed in the whole three
thousand—but I took the cash and put in a check
instead.''

Groucho's Idea

Groucho Marx was married to a Gentile woman.
When his son was about ten years old he took him
to the pool of a restricted country club. The attendant, obviously embarrassed but under firm orders,
told Groucho that neither he nor his son could be
admitted. Groucho shot back, ''The kid's only half
Jewish—couldn't he just dunk up to his belly
button?''

Graham's Disciple

No one doubts that the Reverend Billy Graham is
one of the world's greatest orators. People who
have heard him claim he is absolutely spellbinding.

One evening, Sam Levine, an elderly, strictly
Orthodox Jew, decided to go to Madison Square
Garden to hear Billy Graham. He had been reading
about this man's speaking skills, and he wanted to
hear him for himself. He had also heard that Graham was a strong friend of Israel and the Jewish
community.

The garden was packed, as it always is when
Graham speaks. Sam sat in one of the seats close
to the rostrum, and within a half hour he was
virtually mesmerized. When Graham dramatically

announced that all those who wished to pledge their lives to Jesus should step forward, Sam found himself walking toward Graham.

When he came home later that evening, his wife, Tilly, was already in bed, half asleep. As he undressed, Sam announced, "From now on, we're becoming Christians. I heard Billy Graham, and he convinced me."

Tilly mumbled, "Okay, okay, but go to sleep already. It's late."

Sam awoke at six the next morning, as he had been doing all his life. He washed and then, before breakfast, donned his *tallit* (prayer shawl) and *tefillin* (phylacteries), and with his prayer book in hand began to recite the morning service as he had been doing for nearly a half-century.

Tilly was fixing breakfast and saw her husband in the living room, transfixed in prayer. Her tone a little derisive, she called out, "Sam, I thought you said last night we were becoming Christians."

Sam stopped in mid-prayer. He slapped his forehead in a gesture of self-disgust. "You see," he shouted, "already I have a *goyishe kop* (Gentile head)!"

How to Tell

A rabbi, a Protestant minister, and a Catholic priest were walking home one evening from an ecumenical meeting. On a quiet side street they were startled to see, through an open window, a couple making love. The priest said, "They can't be one of ours—there's no crucifix on the wall." The minister said, "Not one of ours either—no Bible's on the shelf."

The rabbi, embarrassed, conceded the couple must be Jewish. Both of his colleagues asked how he could be so sure. "Easy," he replied, "wall-to-wall carpeting."

Ecumenical Choice

A rabbi and a priest were seated on a plane in adjoining seats. The stewardess asked the rabbi if he'd like a cocktail, and the rabbi said he'd love a Manhattan. When the priest was asked the same question, he said, "I'd just as soon commit adultery as drink an alcoholic beverage." The rabbi quickly chimed in, speaking to the stewardess, "As long as there's a choice, I'll have what he's having," indicating the priest.

"Friendly" Jews

The Protestant and Catholic clergymen in a small midwestern town had become alarmed by the growing number of people who were becoming Quakers. Also known as the Society of Friends, the Quakers had managed to attract both young and old people to their faith.

One day the leading Episcopalian called an emergency meeting of all the Christian clergymen in town. He did not invite the rabbi, with whom he was quite friendly, because he assumed that the

Quakers had not made any inroads into the small Jewish community.

Therefore, when the rabbi knocked on the minister's door later that evening, the Episcopalian was surprised. "Why, Rabbi," he said, "I didn't realize you were having problems also."

To which the rabbi swiftly retorted: "Oh, yes," he said, "some of my best Jews are Friends."

A Horse and a Hat

Morris Silverman and his Gentile friend, John Russell, loved to bet on the horses. One day, John, back from a trip to Florida, told his pal Morris a tale of woe:

"I went to the track in Hialeah, and the first thing I noticed there was a horse in the first race called Beret—it sounded good to me, so I put down a hundred dollars and, guess what—it came in, at ten to one! So now I'm hot. In the second race I see there's a horse called Derby, so naturally I plunk down all of my money, all the winnings, and Lady Luck was with me—again the horse came in first, and the odds were eight to one, and I cleaned up!

"So now, I'm feeling invincible. I look at the third race, and there's a horse called Chateau—you know, French for hat. I put the money down again—"

"Wait a minute. *Chateau* doesn't mean hat—the word is *chapeau*."

"Yeah, now I know, but at the time I didn't

know. Anyway, all my money is on this nag, and she came in last—I lost every dime!''

Morris shared his friend's tale of sorrow. ''So, tell me, which horse did win in the third?''

''Oh, some filly with a Japanese name—yarmulke.''

Monetary Policy

A rabbi, a priest, and a minister were on a train together, talking about their respective congregations and vocations. The rabbi said that synagogues don't have collection plates but that many of them have an alms box—a *pushke*—into which donations can be placed.

The minister said he usually drew a circle on the floor of his office, and then tossed the proceeds from the collection plate into the air. ''Whatever lands to the right of the circle is for God, and the rest is for me.'' The priest said he did virtually the same thing. Then the rabbi added: ''I do it a little differently—I toss the money up in the air, and whatever God catches, He keeps—the rest is for me.''

Star of David

An American Air Force unit was stationed in Saudi Arabia, a number of years prior to the Persian Gulf crisis precipitated by Iraq's invasion of Kuwait. The Saudis did not permit Jews into their country; it was a little-known policy of the Pentagon to exclude Jewish men or women from serving in Saudi Arabia.

One day an NCO was in the showers when he noticed one of his men toweling himself after a shower. What caught his eye was the young soldier's ID dog tags—attached to the chain was a fairly large Star of David, the symbol of Judaism and of Israel.

"Jim, what the hell is that you're wearing?" the sergeant asked, pointing to the six-pointed star.

"Oh, that. I just got back from R and R in Germany, I met this terrific Jewish girl—she works in the American embassy—and she gave it to me before I came back here."

"Come on now, you know damn well you can't wear that thing here."

"Bull! I'm an American soldier, I'm serving on an American base, and I'll wear anything that I damn please."

A week later the soldier with the Jewish star was reassigned. He was flown to an American base in Germany.

And two weeks later, virtually every American soldier on that base sported a Star of David.

"Get off the Grass"

Three friends, a Jew, a Pole, and a Spaniard, worked in a factory in Cleveland, and one Sunday they met in the park for a picnic.

The Spaniard said: "I come here often, and when the policeman sees me, he always calls out, 'Hey, Columbus, how're you doing?' "

The Pole said: "He knows me too, and he always calls me Copernicus."

The Jew laughed. "I often come here, and sometimes I stretch out on the grass, and the cop always says the same thing—'Jesus Christ, get off the grass!' "

Nice Jewish Girl

It is a well-established fact that when people convert to another religious faith they usually become more scrupulously observant of the new faith's rules and regulations than people who were born into that particular religion.

A Jewish motherly type, whose son had married a former Gentile girl who had converted to Judaism, was visiting the young couple. The mother-in-law looked upon her daughter-in-law with genuine affection, and marveled at how easily she had adjusted to Jewish rituals and religious rules.

The young couple and the older lady were all having chicken-salad sandwiches for lunch, and the older woman asked her daughter-in-law if she could have a glass of milk. The young woman was taken aback by the request. "Oh, no," she replied, "you know we can't mix meat and milk foods." The mother-in-law felt sheepish, but said nothing until the younger woman left the room for a moment. She then turned to her son and said, "You *shmegueguee*! You couldn't marry a nice Jewish girl!"

Smart Herring

Two women secretaries have worked together for a number of years in a large, busy office. One, Shirley, is Jewish, and the other, Nancy, is not. Over the years Nancy has told her friend that she admires the Jews, for their intelligence and cleverness. One day at lunch, Nancy keeps annoying Shirley, asking her to reveal the "secret" of the Jews' being so smart.

Shirley finally tells her friend and colleague: "Look, if I tell you, you must promise not to tell anyone else." Nancy quickly agrees. "All right," Shirley says, lowering her voice conspiratorially. "The secret is the herring—if you eat a matjes herring every Thursday at breakfast, you'll be smart too."

Nancy is overwhelmed. "Tomorrow is Thursday, bring me a piece, please, Shirley, I'll pay you whatever you say," she pleads.

"All right, I'll bring you some herring tomorrow—it'll cost you ten dollars."

The next morning, Nancy hands over the money and takes the herring from Shirley. Surreptitiously she eats the fish at her desk. During her lunch break she goes out for a walk, passes an appetizing store, goes in, and notices that the price of matjes herring is only $1.89 a pound. When she returns to the office, she confronts Shirley, and demands that she hand back the ten dollars.

Shirley smiles, gives her friend the ten-dollar bill, and says, "See? You're getting smarter already."

Formerly Jewish

The scene is a very WASPy country club in exurbia. Three men who had been born Jews and had converted to Christianity were having a drink together, and discussing the reasons for their conversion. Said one: "I did it for love—I fell in love with Susan, and she said she would marry me if I became a Christian." The second man said, "My reason was pragmatic—I wanted to get somewhere in the legal profession. If I didn't become a Christian, I don't think I would have been named a federal judge."

The third man said: "I did it for a very simple reason—I really believe that Christian teaching is superior to that of Judaism."

The other two men were shocked. They stared at their friend and in almost one breath said: "Are you serious? What do you take us for—a couple of goyim?"

Uninvited Guests

The temperature outside was frigid; snow was falling heavily, and two elderly Jews, Meyer and Saul, found themselves seated in the back row of a large, warm Catholic church. They had been looking for work and had been told to try again the next day. The two men noticed that in front of the church there were a number of women, all dressed in white bridal gowns, and some kind of ceremony was taking place.

Suddenly it occurred to Meyer what was taking place—the women were being formally inducted as nuns.

Meanwhile, a priest detached himself from the group in front of the sanctuary and approached the two Jews seated in the rear. He said, "Pardon me, but may I ask what brings you here today?"

Meyer smiled at him: "It's all right, Father," he said. "We're from the groom's side."

A Rabbi, a Priest, a Bet

Father Reilly and Rabbi Ginsberg had been friends for some thirty years. One evening, the two were playing chess in the rabbi's study, while the rabbi's wife was out for the evening, chairing a Hadassah meeting.

"Abe, tell me straight," the Catholic priest asked his friend, "have you never really tasted bacon or pork?"

The rabbi smiled. "Never," he said.

Reilly continued: "Just between you and me, let's make a little wager—I'll go and know a woman, in the biblical sense, if you promise me you'll have a plate of bacon and eggs. And then we'll compare notes."

Ginsberg smiled, looked to be sure his friend was serious, and said, "Okay, let's meet here again in a month. As you say, we'll compare notes."

A month passed, and on the evening that Mrs. Ginsberg was again out, busy with her local Hadassah chapter, the rabbi and the priest got together again, ostensibly to play chess at the rabbi's home.

Father Reilly spoke first: "Well, Abe, how was it? The bacon, I mean—it wasn't so bad, now, was it?"

The rabbi smiled. "No, John, it wasn't, I have to admit—it reminded me of *gribenes* that my mother used to make, from chicken. But what about you? Did you—?"

For a moment, Father Reilly looked embarrassed. A touch of color appeared in his cheeks. "Well," he said, "I have to admit—it beats bacon."

Grace After Meals

Paul Swenson had been a devoted and productive employee of Solomon Metzger's store for many years. Over the years Swenson had learned about the various Jewish holidays, the rules and traditions for observing the Sabbath, the Jewish view of life after death, and many other tidbits about Jews and Judaism. A bachelor, he was thrilled when one Friday his employer invited him home for a traditional Friday evening Sabbath dinner.

Paul felt at home the moment he stepped over the Metzgers' threshold. He saw the lit candles, the *chalah* loaves on the table, the white napery, the decanter of wine, and the scrubbed, shining faces of the Metzger children.

After the recitation of kiddush over the wine, and the special blessing for the chalah, the meal began, and Paul thoroughly enjoyed the traditional gefilte fish, chicken soup with noodles, roast chicken with vegetables, applesauce dessert, and tea and cake. When the table was cleared, the

Metzger family joined together in singing the grace after meals.

"Can I ask a question?" Paul said to his boss. "You know, with us, we say grace before the meal, and you do it afterward. Why is that?"

Metzger doffed his yarmulke; a tiny twinkle appeared in his eye. "Well, Paul," he said, "it's like this. You pray before you eat, because your meal is not kosher, so you hope you'll get up from the table in one piece. We serve a strictly kosher meal, so we know it's good for you, and afterward we merely thank God for His bounty."

Free Haircuts

A Catholic priest went to the barbershop that had just opened in town. After cutting the priest's hair, the barber declined payment, explaining that "I don't take money from men of the cloth." The next day the priest sent the barber a bottle of Johnny Walker.

A few days later the local Protestant minister came into the shop for a haircut, and again the barber declined payment and explained why. The minister, on the following day, sent the barber a lovely plant for the shop.

The next week the rabbi came in for a haircut, and again the barber refused to accept any payment. So, the next week the rabbi sent the barber— another rabbi to get a free haircut.

Just the Two

Morris Feldstein was the only Jewish patient in the Catholic hospital. He had taken ill while on a sales trip, and was now recovering from emergency surgery. Atop his bed was a crucifix featuring Jesus as he appeared on the cross.

After a few days, a local rabbi, after being informed that there was a Jewish patient in the hospital, came to pay a sick call. He sat at Morris's bedside, learning where the patient came from, what he did for a living, about his family, and about the emergency surgery he had just undergone.

"Tell me," the rabbi asked the patient, "are there any other Jews besides you in the hospital?"

Morris smiled. He pointed to the crucifix above his head and said, "Just Him and me."

A Proud Jew

Two men were seated at a bar, drinking and glancing at the oversize television set above the bartender's post. The news was on, and a picture of Henry Kissinger, then the Secretary of State, appeared on the screen. The older man, Martin Jacobowitz, was a proud Jew. He turned to his neighbor and said, with a tone of admiration, "He's one of ours."

The second man stared at the TV. "What do you mean?" he asked.

"Oh, I mean, he's Jewish, and I'm—well, that makes me proud."

The televised news continued, and soon there

was a sports segment, featuring a retrospective of Sandy Koufax, once the star pitcher of the Brooklyn Dodgers. The Jewish customer at the bar could not restrain himself. "He's one of ours too," he said, practically beaming. The other man nodded.

There then followed a snippet about the opening of a new operatic season, highlighting commentary by Beverly Sills. Again, the Jewish customer became excited. He nudged his neighbor, and with a broad grin said, "She's one of ours too." Now the neighbor was annoyed. He turned to Jacobowitz and made no effort to disguise his annoyance. "Jesus Christ!" he yelled. "Enough already!" And Jacobowitz, in a somewhat softer voice, shot back, "He's one of ours too!"

Three Questions

Rabbi Moscowitz and Father Flanagan had been friends for more than thirty years. One evening they were alone, relaxing in a quiet restaurant where they had both enjoyed a sumptuous meal.

"Nathan," the priest said, bending toward his friend as they both lit up expensive-looking cigars, "I want to ask you something—you know, about Judaism. Mind?"

"No, not at all, Peter. Ask away."

"Fine. Now, why is it if you enter a synagogue, there seems to be a lot of noise when people pray, not like in the church—where you can hear a pin drop.

"Also, whenever I hear of a young Jewish woman who becomes pregnant out of wedlock, you

77

people carry on like it's the end of the world. And one more question that has been troubling me—at a Jewish funeral, people carry on, they cry and wail, it's terrible. You have to admit that our wakes and funerals are much more orderly.

"Now, then, your comments, please, Nathan."

The rabbi puffed on his cigar, thought for a moment, and then responded: "Your first question—yes, you're right, our services are noisier, people do talk louder, but that's because our God is older, and He's a little hard of hearing. As to the unmarried young Jewish women who are with child—well, you know, there was such a young lady, a long time ago, she gave birth in ancient Judea, and we're still being blamed for that whole event. As to the funerals, Peter, you are absolutely correct—yours are much more decorous, and I would rather go to one of yours than one of ours!"

Up to Her Chin

Mary Flanagan met and fell in love with Jacob Wasserman. The two seemed to be perfectly matched for each other, and when Jacob suggested that Mary convert to Judaism, she readily agreed.

In accordance with established procedures, she attended classes in the synagogue for a half-year, learning Jewish history, culture, philosophy, customs and ceremonies, holiday celebrations and ritual observances. When she was tested by the rabbi, she passed with flying colors.

"Now, all you have to do is go to the mikvah, for the ritual of immersing yourself in fresh water,

78

and after that, we'll make it official and you will be a full-fledged Jew," the rabbi told her.

Excited, Mary went to the beauty parlor and asked for the most expensive and elaborate hair treatment they had. When she left the salon, she positively glowed and looked stunning. At the mikvah, the elderly lady attendant helped her out of her clothes and guided her to the special ritual pool. Gingerly, Mary—whose Hebrew name would soon be Sarah—entered the water and dunked herself—but only up to her chin.

The attendant called out, "No, no, the law is, you have to put your head under the water also, just for a minute."

"But I just spent fifty dollars for this hairdo," Mary protested. "Please, call the rabbi and ask him if it's okay if I just go up to my chin. I'll wait here."

The attendant nodded and called the rabbi. She returned after what seemed like an interminable period of time. She called out to Mary, "The rabbi says, all right, up to your chin, but he wants you to know that you'll be Jewish, yes, but because you didn't wet your head also, you'll always have a *goyishe kop* (Gentile head)."

◆◆◆◆◆◆◆◆◆◆ 4 ◆◆◆◆◆◆◆◆◆◆

Through a Rabbinical Prism

The word *rabbi* has come to signify the Jewish version of a priest or minister. It is that too, but the original meaning of the word is that of *teacher*—and in ancient and medieval times, the rabbi became the leader of the community because he was the most learned, the most knowledgeable, and therefore the best equipped to lead.

Rabbis today are still primarily teachers, interpreters, advisers, leaders. Sometimes they are inspirational. And at all times, they are human, just like the rest of us.

Uncommon Eulogy

Like most ethnic minorities, Jews are embarrassed by fellow Jews who are criminals, slum landlords, and generally bad people, and they are inordinately proud of Jews who help to advance science and medicine, contribute to art and culture, and make this world a better place to live in for everybody.

Thus, when the rabbi of a Chicago synagogue was approached by the family of a known mobster and was asked to deliver a eulogy and conduct the service at the man's funeral, the rabbi declined. The mobster's widow would not take no for an answer; she pointed out to him that her children would be humiliated for life if there was no service. So, out of a sense of compassion for the man's family, the rabbi agreed.

There were perhaps a dozen people in the chapel that could hold two hundred people ordinarily. The rabbi stood on a raised platform, the closed casket in front of him. The man's widow and their two children were in a front row. A few older men and women appeared to be the widow's family or friends.

Perhaps for the first time in his life the rabbi was at a loss for words. The decedent had been imprisoned numerous times; his name had been linked with various criminal activities; the rabbi had actually never met him, although he knew both the widow and the children, who would come to services from time to time, and who had been pointed out to him on several occasions.

The rabbi read the traditional prayers for the newly deceased, first in Hebrew and then in English. He took his glasses off, and stared down at the tiny group.

"One thing I'll say," the rabbi declared, "his brother was worse!"

Rabbi and Cabbie

Two people died in Israel, one a rabbi and the other a taxi driver. As it happened they had been neighbors in Jerusalem and had known each other for a number of years. Luckily, both were good men and they met again in what Jews often refer to as the "heavenly abode."

The first thing the rabbi noticed was that his friend from earth now lived in a beautiful, spacious home, while he had been given what to all intents and purposes was a shack.

Never at a loss for words, the rabbi sought out the authorities and complained bitterly. "Was I not a good man?" he demanded. "Did I not work all my life to do God's work? Is this my just reward?"

There was a brief consultation among the heavenly authorities, and then one of them spoke:

"Rabbi, the facts speak for themselves. The record shows that when you preached, everyone slept. And when the taxi driver drove, all his passengers prayed hard."

Switching Places

One of the great rabbinical scholars of the nineteenth century was a certain Rabbi Moshe the Wise. His erudition and learning were universally respected and admired. Rabbi Moshe did not have a permanent pulpit of his own; instead, he would travel from town to town, from hamlet to hamlet, where he would stay for a few days or a week, and there he would teach and preach and respond to religious questions that might have arisen during the elapsed time from his previous visit.

His traveling companion was a *baal-agolah*, literally a wagon driver, and generally a simple, uneducated man. In the case of Rabbi Moshe, the driver was uneducated, but he also envied Rabbi Moshe's position in the community. Whenever the two of them arrived in a community, the rabbi was treated almost royally, provided with a comfortable room, given the finest meal available, and in general made a big fuss over. The driver on the other hand was often provided with a place to sleep in the stable, and given a perfunctory meal. After many years together, the driver one day voiced his frustration and envy to Rabbi Moshe.

"I tell you what, Mendel," the rabbi said to his driver. "In the next town they don't know me. I've never been there before, they only know about me. Let's change places—you take my coat and hat, take my place when we get there, I'll pretend to be your driver, and who knows—maybe you're right, you'll be able to teach and answer the questions just like I do."

The wagon driver was delighted. He could not believe his good fortune and the rabbi's willingness to switch roles. In the morning they set out, the rabbi doing the driving, and the wagon driver sitting in the back, acting like the rabbi.

When they arrived at their destination, they were both escorted into the local inn's dining room, where they were welcomed warmly by the leaders of the community. The wagon driver-turned-rabbi was seated at the main table, surrounded by the local rabbi and the principal supporters of the synagogue and religious school, while the rabbi-turned-wagon driver was seated in a corner together with some obviously poor people. A bottle of cheap vodka was placed in front of him, it being assumed that wagon drivers enjoyed strong drink.

For a time everyone was busy eating, which of course was followed by the traditional *benching,* or grace. Finally, the rabbi of the town rapped for silence. All eyes in the room turned to him. In a loud voice, he faced the visiting "rabbi" sitting alongside him, and said:

"Honored rabbi, we have waited for your arrival for nearly ten months. A question has arisen in our study of the tractate Bava Metzee'a in the Talmud that no one in our community can understand. But now that you are here, thank God, we will have it explained to us."

And with that, he read aloud a Talmudic passage, not more than thirty words long, in the original Aramaic, while the "rabbi" nearby stroked his beard and listened intently.

The local rabbi, almost plaintive now, asked for a commentary and an explication. The eyes of each person in that room were now focused on the driver-turned-rabbi. They could not wait to hear his words of wisdom, for after all, was he not one of the great sages of the ages?

For a moment the driver-turned-rabbi was deep in thought. And then he smiled and looked relaxed. Without a moment's hesitation he said:

"My dear friends, the answer is so plain, so

obvious, that even my wagon driver can answer it. Mendel, tell them the answer!''

Not a Doctor

Many rabbis have earned their Ph.D.s, in addition to their rabbinical ordination, known as *s'meecha*. Some rabbis like to be called Doctor so-and-so, instead of Rabbi so-and-so; others actually prefer to be known as Rabbi Dr. so-and-so.

In one Westchester synagogue there was a rabbi who wanted to be known as Rabbi so-and-so, even though he had earned a Ph.D. One of the active members of the temple's sisterhood believed it was much more prestigious to address him as Dr. And one day, he became annoyed with this lady, who seemed to gravitate to fancy airs and titles. ''Please,'' the rabbi admonished her, ''I'm not a doctor—I'm not even a nurse!''

A Rabbi Complains

The rabbi's daughter had been married for only three months. Once the young couple visited the rabbi and his wife, and after they left, the rabbi turned to his wife and said:

''*Oy vay,* our son-in-law doesn't know a thing about drinking and card playing!''

''So, why do you say 'Oy vay.' Lots of people I know wish that their sons-in-law didn't know anything about cards and drinking.''

''Yes, but you don't understand. Our son-in-law

doesn't know, but he keeps on drinking and he keeps on playing!''

Not a Prophet

A young immigrant arrived in America in the early years of the twentieth century. He settled in a small town in Iowa, where a cousin lived, and immediately began to look for work. Since he had a pleasant voice and the small synagogue in town did not have a permanent rabbi or cantor, he became a cantor and conducted services for a small salary. After a while, he also became the community's shochet, the ritual slaughterer who provided kosher meat and poultry to the community.

After a few years, since he already was serving as a cantor and shochet, the community designated him as a rabbi, and now he held all three positions.

One day a congregant stopped him on the street and asked what was the name of the biblical portion that would be read in the synagogue on the upcoming Sabbath. Now the rabbi-cantor-shochet got annoyed. He said to his congregant:

"I may be your rabbi-cantor-shochet, but I am not a prophet! I don't know the answer to your question, and I refuse to prophesy."

No One Perfect

The leaders of the congregation approached the rabbi, who had recently hired a new cantor for the synagogue.

"Rabbi," the trustees said, "our people don't like the new cantor."

The rabbi nodded and then responded: "Look, my friends, a cantor must have four traits—first, he must know the Torah, second, he must be an observant Jew, third, he must be a man of integrity, and fourth, he has to be able to sing. Now you know he possesses the first three—and you should understand, that in this world nobody can have everything!"

A Sexton Fails

A rabbi and a sexton, usually called a shamash, had worked together in a suburban synagogue for more than thirty years. One day, after a minor tiff between the two men over a petty issue, the rabbi fired the sexton, who left the synagogue in a huff.

A proud man, if not the most learned or the wisest in the world, the sexton walked toward the local Catholic church. He had heard that the sexton had been retired, and believed he could do the job, just as he had been doing it in the synagogue. Without too much ado, he approached the priest and applied for the opening.

The priest was looking for a new sexton, and wondered to himself if this Jewish gentleman could fill the opening. He said to him, "Well, you have to know something about our religion. Tell me, where was Jesus born?" The Jewish sexton did not have a clue but made a stab at the answer. "Philadelphia?" The priest dismissed him, and the shamash now proceeded to the Protestant church in town.

Again he approached the minister in charge, explained that he was looking for a position, and adding that after a quarter-century of service in the synagogue he felt he could perform his duties well. And again the Protestant minister agreed that there was an opening, and that if he were to get the job, he would have to know something about the Christian religion.

"Tell me," the minister asked the shamash, "do you know where Jesus was born?"

The shamash appeared to be thinking hard, and this time he replied, "Pittsburgh?" The minister politely sent him away, and the shamash found himself walking back toward the synagogue. Feeling contrite, he went to the rabbi, apologized for their misunderstanding, the rabbi excused him, and rehired him on the spot. It had been a painful day for the sexton.

"Tell me, Rabbi," the shamash asked, "where was Jesus born?"

"Bethlehem," the rabbi responded.

"Damn! I knew it was in Pennsylvania," the sexton said, and went home.

Sleepers Offered

An ad appeared in a major Toronto newspaper. The Canadian railroad authorities were seeking bids for two hundred sleepers. A phone number and the name of a Mr. Adams were included in the announcement.

On the day following publication of the ad, Mr. Adams was surprised to receive a phone call from a local rabbi, who said quite simply: "You need two hundred sleepers? You can have my entire congregation."

Arrival of Poor

A rabbi in Houston got up before his congregation on Saturday morning, at the weekly Sabbath service. Speaking in a modulated tone, he said: "I have always preached that the poor are always welcome in this house of God." Then he paused, looked about him slowly, and said: "Judging from our receipts last month, they have all come."

Send for Priest

Zalman the elderly Hebrew schoolteacher lay dying. He was now past ninety, and the heart attack he had suffered four days ago was massive. His wife of more than sixty years was at his bedside, holding his hand, trying to ease his pain and to give him moral support. Outside their modest home the elements seemed to have gone crazy. Lightning flashed through the sky, thunderclaps reverberated one after the other, and the rain was truly torrential.

Faintly, Zalman said to his wife, "Goldie, send for a priest. I think it's the end."

She stared at him. "Zalman, you mean, send for a rabbi."

"No, I said a priest. A rabbi should go out on a night like this?"

"Anti-Semitism"

A congregant went to see his rabbi. "R-R-Rabbi, th-th-there is anti-S-Sem-Semitism in A-A-Ame-me-rica," he said. "I we-went fo-for a jo-job—th-they would'nt e-e-even gi-give me a ch-cha-chance."

"What kind of job was it?" the rabbi asked.

"R-Ra-Radio an-noun-noun-cer."

Marine Solution

The time is the year 2089. The world's leading scientists have sadly announced that all the oceans of the world would engulf all of the continents in three days. Universal pandemonium breaks out. In Rome the Pope goes on international television, urging people to accept Jesus, assuring them that it is not too late. A similar spiritual message is televised from India by a major Buddhist leader.

From Jerusalem, the chief rabbi of Israel goes on the air. His message is short and to the point: "We have three days in which to learn to live under water!"

Stepping Up

A rabbi and a priest who had been close friends for many years were relaxing with a few bottles of beer. The priest asked the rabbi, "Abe, you ever feel like moving up in the world?" The rabbi thought for a moment. "Well, John, I used to think of trying to serve in a bigger congregation, but lately I'm feeling very content right here. What about you?"

"Well, I have thought of what it would be like to be a cardinal." The priest pondered a little and then added: "In theory at least I could even aspire to become the Pope."

"And after that?" the rabbi asked.

"What do you mean 'after that'? You want me to become God?"

"Well, as you know, one of our boys did make it."

The Poor Agree

The poor rabbi in the shtetl was finished with his morning prayers. As he put his prayer shawl and prayer book away, his shrewish wife asked him, "Well, what did you pray for this morning?"

"I prayed that God would persuade the rich to give larger donations to the poor."

"And do you think God will pay attention to your prayers?"

"Well, one thing I'm sure of—half of the prayer is already answered. The poor people have agreed to accept larger donations."

Foolish Congregant

A congregant made an appointment to see the rabbi. When he sat down in the rabbi's book-lined study, he was obviously nervous and upset.

"What's the problem, Mr. Bloom?" the rabbi asked.

"Well, I'll come straight to the point—there are certain members of the synagogue who call me a fool."

"But why should that bother you?"

"I don't like to be called that—it's insulting."

"Look, fools are just like everybody else. In fact, some of my best friends are fools. I think that even you, a wise, fine man, could also be a fool. So what?"

A Proud Death

A shtetl rabbi learns that a member of his congregation has died, and when told that the man died of hunger, he is shocked.

"It can't be!" the rabbi exclaims. "If we had known that he was in need, we would have provided food for him."

"Rabbi, he was too embarrassed to ask for help," a congregation trustee says. "He was very proud."

"Aha!" the rabbi said. "Now, that's more like it—he died of pride, not hunger."

Righteous Compromise

Two diametrically opposed schools of Talmudic thought are represented by the names of Hillel and Shamai. The latter was generally a stern, strict interpreter of the law, while the former was usually far more lenient and gentle in his views.

Adherents of each school once argued for a long time over whether it was good that mankind had been created; Shamai's people thought it was better for mankind not to have been created, while Hillel's followers insisted that the creation of mankind was a good thing. Finally, the two groups compromised on the issue: Yes, it would have been better if man had not been created, but since he was, it was desirable to make the best of it, and conduct a righteous life.

Sage Advice

Three stern-faced congregational trustees met with the rabbi of their synagogue, in the Hassidic section of Brooklyn known as Boro Park.

Their spokesman launched right in. "Rabbi, what shall we do—the young girls in our community, our daughters, are beginning to dress just like everybody else. Their necklines are getting deeper, and their hems are getting higher. What shall we do?"

"Don't look," the rabbi advised.

A Rabbi Yells

Rabbi Leibowitz was known far and wide as a kind, compassionate person who never raised his voice against anyone. His congregants felt only great sympathy for him because of his wife, who was a shrew and whose sharp words had injured many people. One day, after the rabbi's wife had berated him for some trifling matter, he was heard to yell back at her, and reject her criticism.

Later that day, the *shamash,* the beadle, who was very close to the rabbi, asked him privately what had made him finally talk back.

The rabbi sighed and smiled simultaneously: "Well, I thought it would have been cruel of me to remain silent—I knew she wanted to hear me yelling back at her. So I did!"

Miracle Deed

Two Hassidic Jews were extolling the miracle powers of their respective rabbis. One man said:

"Look, my rabbi saw a Jew, a neighbor, eating ham and eggs, and of course he became incensed. He cursed the man, and said he hoped the house in which the man lives would collapse.

"But then, after a few minutes he had second thoughts. What if there were innocent, God-fearing people living in the same house? So, he rescinded his original curse and said he hoped the house would not collapse and fall down."

"So?"

95

"So look at the house, it's still standing—it's a miracle!"

Preacher Explains

An itinerant preacher was in the village congregation one weekday evening. When he concluded his formal lecture, he appealed to the congregants for funds for "a poor widow with seven children."

Some of the congregants wanted to know who the unfortunate woman was, and the preacher explained: "Actually, she is my wife and the seven children are also mine."

"But she's not a widow! You're lying!" a number of congregants shouted at the preacher.

"So—what are you saying? You begrudge one Jew a chance to live in this world?"

IRS Probes

An investigator for the Internal Revenue Service was ushered into the study of the rabbi, who served a wealthy congregation in an affluent New York suburb.

"Rabbi, one of your congregants, Donald Markowitz, claims that he donated five thousand dollars to the synagogue. Is this true?" the IRS man asked.

The rabbi smiled, and then laughed, and replied: "Well, no, not yet—but it will be, believe me."

Dying Comment

The aged and revered rabbi of the Boston congregation was on his deathbed. Nearby were the members of his family and two of the many students he had been guiding in the local rabbinical school. One of the two rabbis-to-be, speaking softly, said to the rabbi, "Please, before it is too late, give us a parting word of wisdom, to remember you by." The elderly rabbi whispered to his two young disciples: "The Jewish people are like twin stars in the firmament."

He then lay back, his eyes closed, his breathing obviously difficult. One of the two students turned to the other: "What did he mean?" The other shook his head. "I don't know," he said. Without a word, they bent forward to their teacher, and gently asked, "Rabbi, what did you mean about the twin stars?"

The rabbi opened his eyes, stared at his students, and a note of annoyance entered his voice. He said: "All right, all right, the Jewish people are not like the twin stars."

Lost Wallet

The rabbi and the cantor are in the former's study, when the cantor poses a question to the rabbi.

"Tell me," he says, "what would you do if you were walking down the street and you found a wallet with a million dollars?"

"Well, if it belonged to Rothschild, I think I'd be tempted to keep it," the rabbi replied. "What does a million, more or less, mean to him? But, if the wallet belonged to a poor man, I would rush to return it at once, and fulfill the mitzvah of returning a lost article.''

Paradise

A great Talmudic scholar and sage died and went to Paradise. There he discovered many of his colleagues deep in the study of the Talmud. He expressed his amazement to an angel that "this is just like life on earth." "Silly man," the angel said. "You think the sages are in Paradise but in reality, Paradise is in the sages."

5

Czarist or Soviet, Russia Is Russia

In the early years of the twentieth century the overwhelming majority of the Jewish people lived in czarist Russia. They suffered cruel persecutions, including infamous massacres, and as soon as they could, they fled—mostly to the United States, some to Western European countries and South America, and a few hardy souls to Palestine, where they laid the groundwork for the eventual creation of Israel.

Nowadays, a modern miracle has emerged: Although the Soviets suppressed any and all aspects of Judaism for some seventy years, at the first signs of freedom, vast numbers of Soviet Jews who knew nothing of their religious or cultural heritage surfaced and made their way to Israel and to the west, to renew their lives as Jews.

Rabbinical Solution

In a shtetl of Russia, in the middle of the last century, a young father and husband who supported his wife and five children by delivering milk awoke one morning early to discover that his mare had died during the night. It was a disaster! What will he do now? He ran, despite the snow on the ground and the darkness of the night, and came to the home of the rabbi, a much-loved and deeply respected man. S'rulik, the milkman, could see that a light was already burning; he was sure the rabbi, even at that early hour, was deep in study.

He knocked on the door, was ushered in, told the rabbi what had happened, and when the rabbi put on his coat and fur hat and ordered him to follow, he did as he was told. For nearly an hour they walked together, single file, watching the sun come up. At the baronial mansion of the local landowner and landlord of virtually all the homes and farms in the region, the rabbi turned in toward the stables, noting that S'rulik followed behind him.

There were eight stalls in the stable, half of them empty. The rabbi said to S'rulik, "Choose a horse, take it, go deliver your milk—I'll stay behind and explain everything. The baron must be out riding."

"But, but that's like stealing, Rabbi," the young father said.

"Am I asking you for an opinion? Just do as I said. Go, hurry."

S'rulik had total trust in his rabbi. He chose a handsome tawny mare and, gripping the reins, he led her out of the stable toward his modest home so that he could shackle her to his two-wheeled cart and start out on his deliveries.

As soon as his congregant departed, the rabbi took a blanket that was used to cover the horses and spread it out in the stall that had just been emptied. He lay down, closed his eyes, and within moments fell asleep.

It could not have been more than an hour when he heard voices. The rabbi looked up, noticed the baron and some friends staring at him, and exclaimed:

"Oh, good heavens! Oh, dear Lord! It's a miracle! I'm a man again! Oh, thank you, God Almighty! Thank you!"

Startled at the rabbi's outburst, the baron demanded, "Who are you? And where is my horse?"

The rabbi arose, brushed himself off, and spoke to the baron:

"Sir, permit me to explain. My name is Rabbi Meir Barnovsky. I am a teacher and a scholar. About a year ago I met a beautiful woman, I knew she was married and I also knew that her husband was traveling and would be away for many weeks. Well, what shall I tell you? We are all mortal. I was conquered by lust, I committed a terrible sin and seduced that dear woman.

"On the way home from her house, as I was walking through the forest, a voice called out to me, straight from heaven. 'Rabbi Meir,' the voice said. 'Shame on you! For your sin, you shall no longer be a man, you will become a horse until such time as I think you are ready to rejoin the community!

"All I remember after that is a clap of thunder and a big bolt of lightning. I think I have been a horse, right here in your stable, and now that God has forgiven me, I am a man again. Hallelujah!" And with that the rabbi set off, heading for the shtetl and his books, leaving the baron and his companions standing in the stable, as though frozen in time.

The Russian aristocrat and his friends were convinced that they had been privy to a true miracle. They could talk about nothing else all through the day.

The next morning the baron rode into town, his destination the village telegraph office. As he began to mount his horse for the trip back to his mansion, he noticed his missing horse, the tawny mare that until yesterday had occupied a stall in his stable. For a moment he stared at the horse, which was now attached to a wagon filled with milk cans. Without hesitation, the baron stepped forward, put his arm around the mare's neck, and whispered into her ear:

"Well, Rabbi, I see you've been fooling around again!"

Negev Rebirth?

Soon after Stalin died, and before he was interred, the then prime minister of Israel, David Ben-Gurion, received a phone call from Moscow. On the line was the new Soviet dictator, Khrushchev.

"Listen, Ben-Gurion," the Russian said, without any preliminaries. "I know our two countries have not always gotten along so well, but I want you to do me a favor, and someday I'll return it."

"All right—what is it?"

"Well, to come straight to the point—I don't want to put Stalin into a fancy bier here in Moscow, like we have of Lenin—I don't need people to come and look at him and maybe compare him with me. Who needs it? So, listen, if we ship the body to you, can you bury it somewhere in the middle of that Negev desert you have, where no one will find him?''

The Israeli premier hesitated only for a moment.

''All right, yes, we can do it,'' he said. ''The only thing is—you know that we're famous for resurrections.''

Czarist Pet

The Russian czar once summoned his Jewish business adviser. He handed him twenty gold coins and instructed that he buy him a dachshund. The Jewish adviser protested, albeit gently: ''Sire, I do not believe it is possible to buy a dachshund suitable for Your Excellency for twenty gold pieces. It will cost at least fifty.'' The czar handed over thirty more coins. ''But remember, I want the very finest dachshund.''

''Of course, Your Excellency, it will be the finest anywhere,'' the Jew replied. As he prepared to leave the czar's presence, he added: ''By the way, sire, exactly what is a dachshund?''

Long Memory

In czarist Russia, where the bulk of the world's Jewish population lived in the latter part of the nineteenth century and the first decades of the twentieth, admission to the university was a dream that few Jews could even aspire to; the government restricted the number of Jews who were accepted each year, and the numbers were painfully small.

The story is told of a pair of candidates, a young Jewish student and a young Christian, who were vying for a single opening at a prestigious school in Moscow. Each youth was to be examined orally by a committee of professors, and the better of the two would be accepted.

The first candidate to be interviewed was the Russian. He walked into the examining room confidently, and after a quarter hour came out, beaming and announcing that he had been accepted. The Jewish youth went storming into the room where the professors still sat.

"I see there is no point to testing me," he shouted. "You've already made up your minds. How come?"

The chairman of the academic group spoke up. "Well, he displayed such a remarkable memory, we decided we just had to have him as a student."

"Really? What's so remarkable about his memory?"

"He told us about events in his life that took place when he was only five years old."

The Jew thought for a moment. "Listen," he said, "that's nothing. My memory goes back to when I was eight days old—and at that time I had a little operation that precluded my ever becoming a student here."

Hebrew in Heaven

A KGB man, in the Stalin era, spotted a Soviet Jew studying a Hebrew grammar. "What's that for?" he demanded.

"For heaven, so I'll be able to speak Hebrew."
The KGB man snorted. "And if you go to hell?"

"Oh, don't worry," the Jew replied. "Russian I already know."

◆◆◆

Ready, Aim, Wait

A whole class of yeshiva teenagers were forcibly conscripted by the czarist army at the beginning of World War I. The Jewish youths surprised and delighted their Russian officers by their marksmanship on the rifle range.

Finally, after a few months of training, the yeshiva boys' unit was sent to the front, where they were to face the German army forces. At dawn, their officer ordered his men to line up, face the German position, and wait for the order to fire. After about a half hour, a long line consisting of nearly one hundred Jewish students now wearing Russian army uniforms stood facing the German lines, their rifles pointed at the enemy, their forefingers on the trigger.

Now the order came. "Fire!" shouted the Russian captain. No one pulled a trigger. The officer raised his voice and shouted again, "Fire!" and again he was met with silence. He rushed toward the line of yeshiva boys, screaming at them. "Why don't you fire, you idiots?" One of the students spoke up:

"Sir, there are men in the way—we might hit them."

Life in Moscow

A KGB man in Moscow stopped a Russian Jew in the street. "What right do you have to live in the Soviet Union?" he demanded.

The Jew answered: "This you call living?"

Saved by Czar

An elderly Jew fell into the Dnieper River in Russia during the time of the czar. He kept shouting, "Help! Help!" to no avail. Then, two czarist policemen happened by, took in the situation, and said to each other, "Ah, it's only a Jew—let him drown!"

The drowning man changed his plea. Now he shouted, loud and clear, "Down with the czar!" The policemen jumped in, rescued him, and then arrested him.

Saved by Murder

Through the centuries anti-Semites in various parts of the world disseminated a terrible calumny against the Jews—they said the Jews kidnapped Christian children and used their blood for ritual purposes, especially for the Passover seder. Hard as it may be to believe, such a blood libel almost erupted in the upstate New York city of Massena, at the beginning of the twentieth century. Fortunately, a missing Gentile child was found unharmed, and the ugly rumor evaporated.

In czarist Russia, which knew pogroms for many decades, the story is told of a Christian girl who had been found murdered. The Jews in this particular shtetl were terrified that the girl's death would lead to all kinds of horrible charges, resulting in death and destruction for the Jewish community.

The Jewish adults in town had gathered in the synagogue for an emergency conference to decide what to do, when suddenly one of the townspeople came rushing in, shouting and beaming: "Good news, my friends! Good news!" There was an immediate hush, as everyone awaited an explanation from the newcomer.

Catching his breath, he finally shouted, "It's all right! The poor girl is Jewish!"

No Red Ink

A Russian Jewish couple, anxious to emigrate to Israel, find themselves separated by bureaucracy. The husband, Abraham, is not allowed to depart the Soviet Union, but his wife and children are given permission to go. Sara, the wife, works out a code with her husband. It is simplicity itself— anytime he writes to her in black ink, she'll know everything is fine, but any letters in red ink mean that everything in the letter is a fabrication.

A few weeks after her arrival in Israel, Sara receives a letter from her husband. Using a black-ink pen, he writes that everything is just fine—there is plenty of food, people are free to say what they want, the clothing being offered is now stylish and inexpensive, and generally speaking, life is good.

107

"There is just one little problem," Abraham adds in a postscript. "I just can't seem to find any red ink anywhere!"

Doctor's Orders

In the era of czarist rule in Russia, Jews were not allowed to live in or even visit the major cities such as Moscow, St. Petersburg, and Kiev without a special permit. Two cousins named Gershowitz were talking on the street in Moscow one day, when they spotted a policeman who seemed to be checking people's permits. One of the cousins, Label, had a permit, but the other, Mendel, did not, and the sight of the policeman obviously upset him.

"What should I do?" he whispered to his cousin.

"Listen," Label said. "I'm going to start running, the cop will chase me, and that's when you get away. He won't bother me, my permit is tiptop."

And with that Label set out, running past the policeman, who quickly gave chase. After about three blocks the policeman caught up with Label, and demanded to see his permit. He examined it carefully, and then returned it.

"This seems to be in order," he said. "Why did you run just now?"

"Oh, my doctor said that a half hour after each meal I should take a fast run, it's good for the circulation."

"But when you saw me running after you, why didn't you stop?"

"Oh, well, I thought your doctor told you the same thing."

Nocturnal Mailman

A Soviet Jew during the 1960s is awakened by a loud knocking on the door of his Moscow apartment. He calls out, "Who is it?" A loud voice responds, "Mailman."

The Jew rises, opens the door, and is not surprised to see two KGB men. One of them asks, "Are you Glatstein?"

"Yes," he says meekly.

"Did you apply for an exit permit to go to Israel?"

"Yes, I did."

"Tell me, do you have enough to eat in the Soviet Union?"

"Yes."

"Your kids get a good Communist education, right?"

"Yes."

"So, why do you want to go leave our country?"

"Why? Because I don't want to live in a country where the mailman knocks on your door at three in the morning."

Only One Complaint

The emigration of hundreds of thousands of Soviet Jews to Israel brought in its wake myriads of social, economic, political, and human problems before the newcomers adjusted to their new surroundings and the new way of life they found in Israel.

In the Soviet Union, the immigrants liked to tell, the government provided homes and jobs, and in Israel everybody had to fend for themselves.

One day, a recent Soviet Jewish newcomer came dashing into the office of the local immigration office. He was obviously agitated. A clerk tried to calm him.

"Why are you upset?" the Israeli official asked. "Don't you like the apartment we prepared for you?"

"Yes, it's okay."

"And the Ulpan school you went to, you learned Hebrew there. How was it?"

"Fine, fine."

"And we got you a store, you're a tailor, and now you have a place to work, you have a sewing machine and material and thread. So tell me, what's bothering you?"

The Soviet Jew yelled back: "So now send me customers!"

◆◆◆◆◆◆◆◆◆◆◆ **6** ◆◆◆◆◆◆◆◆◆◆◆◆

Eating in and Eating Out

Jewish tradition teaches that "you shall eat, you shall be satisfied, and you shall offer a blessing." In the traditional Jewish family the table where the family gathers for a meal is regarded as a small altar, and is a reminder of the sacrificial altars that existed at the time of the Holy Temple.

The Sabbath dining table, especially on Friday evening, has always been seen as a very special place and time when the cares of the world were put aside, and when parents and children and other close relatives and invited guests would dine together, talk freely and fully, chant the special Sabbath melodies, and in effect create a peaceful oasis in time.

A Chutzpah Example

Chutzpah is a Yiddish (and Hebrew) word best translated as unmitigated gall. For example: a defendant brought before a judge after being found guilty of murdering his parents pleads for mercy on the grounds that he is now an orphan—that's chutzpah.

Another kind of chutzpah involves a beggar who beseeches an obviously wealthy man for help, explaining that he is hungry. The rich man hands him a twenty-dollar bill, moved by the beggar's story. An hour later, the rich man enters his favorite restaurant and sees the same beggar enjoying a meal of bagels and lox. He storms over, berating the poor man: "For this I gave you twenty dollars! So you can eat lox and bagels!"

The beggar wipes his mouth and responds: "Listen, my friend. Before I met you, I couldn't even dream of eating bagels and lox. After I met you, with God's help, I can afford it—and now you don't like the idea. All right, TELL ME—WHEN CAN I EAT BAGELS AND LOX, HEH?"

Cheap Bagels

Mrs. Feinstein walked into Eisenberg's bagel shop. "How much is a dozen bagels?" she asked.

"Three dollars and seventy-five cents," Eisenberg replied.

"But Greenberg sells them for two seventy-five a dozen," Mrs. Feinstein said.

"So, go to Greenberg's."

"No, no, he's out of bagels."

"Well, when I'm out of bagels I also sell them for two seventy-five."

Only Two Cents

Mrs. Blatt was shopping in the corner green-grocer's. She was at the cucumber section. "How much are they?" she asked the proprietor.

"Two for five cents."

She hesitated, picked one up, and again asked, "How much is this one?"

"Three cents."

Now she put it back, took the other one, and with a smile said, "Fine, I'll take this one for two cents."

Special Visitor

A member of the Rothschild family traveled through a poverty-stricken shtetl area of Eastern Europe. He stopped at an inn and ordered breakfast, which included two eggs. When the bill came, he was startled to see that the innkeeper had charged him twenty rubles for the pair of eggs. He was clearly annoyed.

"Tell me," he admonished the owner of the inn, "how can you charge so much for two paltry eggs? Are eggs so scarce in these parts?"

"No, not at all, sir," the innkeeper said. "Rothschilds are."

Chalah as a Sponge

A wealthy man invites a poor stranger home for the traditional Sabbath meal. A bottle of cognac is on the table, together with the customary Chalah loaves, fish, meat, and chicken soup.

A small goblet stands alongside the cognac, but the guest ignores it and pours a hefty amount of the strong drink into his saucer and begins to drink it straight, sponging it up with Chalah.

The host comments: "You know, if you lived during Moses' day, he wouldn't have had to split the sea for the Israelites—you could all have soaked up the water with pieces of Chalah."

"No, no," the guest responds, "it wouldn't work—you see, it was Passover, and there was no Chalah, only matzoh, and with matzoh you can't really do any soaking!"

Lucky Few

Two elderly members of B'nai B'rith are seated in a diner, having coffee and waffles after a meeting of their lodge. One of the two says: "I tell you, Sam, to be a Jew, it's not easy—pogroms, anti-Semitism, discrimination, Nazis, the Klan—sometimes it seems we'd be better off not even to be born."

His friend nods, munching on his waffle. "Yeah," he says, "but who has such luck? Maybe one in a hundred thousand?"

Forbidden Apple

Alan Lichtenstein is the president of an Orthodox synagogue in Los Angeles. Although he is observant of Jewish religious laws and customs, from time to time he falls off the wagon, as it were, and goes out of his way to find a remote restaurant where he can eat a meal of roast suckling pig. He knows he shouldn't, but once or twice a year the desire for this food, complete with an apple in the pig's mouth, overcomes him.

One day he feels compelled to eat of the forbidden food. He gets into his car and drives thirty miles to a small town where he is sure no one he knows would ever see him. He enters the restaurant, spots the dish "roast suckling pig" on the menu, orders it, and sits back awaiting its arrival. Suddenly, he blanches as he sees the rabbi enter the restaurant, spot him, and approach his table.

"Rabbi, what are you doing around here?" Lichtenstein asks.

"Driving through, and I just thought I'd better have some coffee and cake before I go on."

At this moment, the waiter returned, placed the roast suckling pig in front of Lichtenstein, and departed. The synagogue president stared at the dish on the table, and then turned to the rabbi. He said:

"What a strange place this is! I ordered an apple, and look how they serve it here!"

No Politics

The scene is a modest restaurant in Moscow in the 1960s, before large-scale Jewish emigration was permitted. A group of three friends are sipping tea and not saying a word. One of them finally groans,

"Oy." The second man, as though on cue, says softly, "Oy, vay," and the third friend nods his head and whispers, "Nu, nu." At which point the first man warns his companions: "Listen, if you're going to talk politics, I'm getting out of here."

Voracious Appetite

An assimilated Jew approached a local Hassidic rabbi. He said that although he almost never observed religious strictures, all his life he had refrained from eating pork—until last week. He explained that he had been at a business convention, and at dinner the only item on the menu was pork, he ate it, and now he felt contrite. What should he do?

The rabbi recommended that he attend daily services for a month, and each morning, at the early service, he should recite a chapter of the Book of Psalms.

The next morning the man was at the morning service, and he began to read the chapter in Psalms that the rabbi had recommended. He could not help but notice that his neighbor, a short man barely five feet tall, was reciting what appeared to be the entire Book of Psalms. He thought to himself as he watched his neighbor race through the ancient text, "My God! It's amazing how much pork this little guy must have eaten!"

Silent Waiter

Morris Abramson was a lonely old bachelor who had taken to having his dinner every evening in the same Jewish restaurant. The only complaint he had about the restaurant was that the waiter was sullen and never uttered a friendly word.

One day Morris appeared, like clockwork, for dinner. The same unsmiling and sullen waiter served him, as he had been doing for a number of years.

Morris ordered one of his favorite dishes, chicken soup with *kreplach*. The waiter brought the dish, silent as ever. "Wait a minute," Morris said. "*Zog a vort,* say something." The waiter faced Morris, his face expressionless. "You want me to say a few words, huh? Okay, okay. Don't eat the *kreplach*."

Sabbath Hour

One of the great rabbinical personalities of the twentieth century is Rabbi Adin Steinsalz of Jerusalem, who has been compared in his scholarship to Maimonides and Rashi. With a twinkle in his eye, he likes to tell about a class in Talmud he gives in Jerusalem, designed for nonreligious adults who would like to study the great biblical commentaries.

"One of these men, a successful businessman and a civic leader," the rabbi recalls, "tried to shock me. Before the class began he said, 'Rabbi, I want you to know I eat bacon on the Sabbath.' I

117

asked him, 'And the rest of the week?' and he replied, 'Oh, the rest of the week I get by on coffee and bread.' So I said to him, 'Well, you honor the Sabbath by eating bacon. I wouldn't do it, but if that's your way, that's it.' "

Mournful Diner

Ben Marcus entered his favorite kosher delicatessen-restaurant. He told the waiter to bring him a plate of roast beef. When the waiter dropped off the plate, Ben was appalled to see how tiny a portion he had been given. Suddenly, he began wailing, tears flowing from his eyes, and everyone in the restaurant stopped to stare at him.

The waiter rushed over, visibly upset.

"What's the matter, Mr. Marcus?" he asked his regular customer. "Is there anything I can do? Why are you crying?"

Marcus wiped his eyes and said to the waiter: "I'm crying because I'm so sad—and I'm sad when I think of the fact that for this tiny piece of beef on my plate, a great big steer had to be killed."

Disappointed Rabbi

A humble, pious, and beloved rabbi died and went, of course, straight to heaven. When his first meal was served he was disappointed but he did not wish to complain. He quietly ate a small piece of herring and a dry piece of bread. From where he sat, the saintly rabbi could see into Gehenna, which most people refer to as hell, and to his astonishment he noticed that the meals being served there were sumptuous feasts—he could almost smell the steaks, chopped liver, fine wines, and pastries.

He turned to the angel with him and noted the difference between the modest meals he and the angel were sharing and the feasts being eaten in hell. The angel looked embarrassed. "I know, I know," he said. "But you see, it doesn't pay to cook for just two people."

Return of the Waiter

Jewish waiter stories practically form a genre of their own. The best-known one of course is the waiter who approaches a packed table, a glass of water in his hand, and asks, "Who ordered a clean glass?"

Then there's the story of Laibel the waiter, who died and who was sorely missed by his customers. Some of these loyal patrons join together and go to a medium, who promises to summon Laibel from the great beyond at a seance.

The customers and the spiritualist are seated around a large table, the room is in semidarkness, and the medium urges her guests to knock on the table, promising that Laibel will appear. The patrons begin to knock and knock, ever louder and louder, and some of them call out the name of Laibel.

And then, there he is, a small handcloth draped over his arm. There is a hush, and finally one of the customers whispers, "Laibel, why didn't you come when we first knocked on the table?"

"It wasn't my table," Laibel replied.

"Taste this Soup"

Max has been patronizing the same restaurant for many years. It's a *haimish* (homey) kind of place, and Max, a bachelor, has been coming in for dinner almost every night for many years.

On this particular evening, after the waiter has placed a bowl of soup before him, he calls over the waiter and says, "Taste this soup."

"No, what for? You don't like it, I'll change it. What shall I bring you?"

"I said, taste this soup."

The waiter grows a little anxious. "Max, you're our very best customer," he pleads. "You're like a member of the family. You don't like the soup, I'll be happy to bring you anything else. No problem. Just tell me what you want."

"Taste this soup!"

The waiter does not recognize the urgent note in Max's voice. "All right," he says, "all right—where's the spoon?"

"AHAH!" Max yells.

He Loves Bread

A new customer sits down in Harry's kosher delicatessen, orders a meal, seems to enjoy it, and when he goes to the register to pay his bill, the owner asks him if he enjoyed dinner. "Fine," he said, "but I could have used a little more bread."

"How many slices of bread did you get?"

"Just two."

"Next time you get four."

A few nights later the new patron appeared, the waiter brought him four slices of bread, the owner-cashier again asked about the meal, and again the customer said he could have used more bread. "Next time, eight slices!"

Sure enough, a few nights later, the customer was back, the eight slices of bread were placed before him as promised, and when the owner again questioned him, the customer again said he could use more bread.

When the newcomer came in next time, the owner told the waiter to take a large loaf of bread, cut it in half, and give the entire loaf to the bread-loving customer.

"So, how was dinner tonight?" the owner asked as the patron was paying his bill.

"Fine, fine, but I see you're back to two pieces of bread."

Chicken Test

Chicken has been a staple of the Jewish family's diet for many generations. The kosher butcher is a quasi-religious institution in most Jewish neighborhoods. One day, a new customer enters the local butcher shop. She nods perfunctorily to the butcher, whose bloodstained apron identifies him vividly. She picks up one chicken, then another, and finally seems to settle on a particular bird.

But now she undertakes a minute examination. She lifts the chicken's wings, and smells underneath; next she spreads the chicken's legs, and again she smells the area carefully. Finally she turns to the butcher.

"Mister," she says, "this is not a good chicken. Show me another one."

The butcher remains in his place, his arms folded. "Lady," he says, "could you pass such a test?"

◆◆◆◆◆◆◆◆◆◆◆ **7** ◆◆◆◆◆◆◆◆◆◆◆

Once Upon a Time, in the Shtetl

Ever since the phenomenal, universal success of *Fiddler on the Roof,* the word *shtetl* has become almost a household word. It means of course a hamlet, a small village often nearly one hundred percent Jewish in makeup, subsisting on local agriculture and such essential businesses as shoe repair, lumberyards, and tailoring. And of course because it was an isolated Jewish community, it often became a center of religious studies and religious devotion. Jews in the shtetl felt safe from hostile mobs, and yet they also felt cheated for being cut off from the mainstream of society and reduced to an underclass without any real rights.

Pregnant Daughter

In the old country it was traditional for affluent families to take in a yeshiva student for a period of

123

a year or six months, and provide room and board so that the student could continue with his religious studies. Sometimes a student would meet a daughter of marriageable age, and a wedding would ensue.

The story is told of an affluent family that brought in such a yeshiva student for a period of six months. He happened to be a very handsome young man of about twenty-one years of age, and the family had three unmarried daughters, ages seventeen, eighteen, and nineteen. While the student was a guest in the house, everything was fine. The people involved all enjoyed one another's company, and the six months passed quickly, after which the young man moved out to live in another house.

At this point, perhaps a month after he left, the middle daughter approached her father privately. With tears streaming down her face, she confessed to him that she was pregnant, and the guilty party was the young student. That very day the father sat down and wrote a sharp, angry letter to the student, notifying him that one of his daughters was pregnant and that he, the student, had better hie back to town, marry the girl, and be a father to the child.

When the student received the father's letter, he was at first a little shocked, but then he thought it over, remembered the pleasant time he had spent in that family's household, and decided to accede to the father's request and marry the girl immediately.

He wrote a letter, expressing his dismay at the news he had just received, and assuring the father that he was making preparations to return at once and get married. And then he added a postscript:

"By the way, which of the girls got pregnant?"

Judicial Decision

Miserliness is a trait frequently derided in Jewish tradition. Generosity is not, however, widely extolled, because it is not viewed as charity, but rather as a righting of a wrong. Thus, the Hebrew word for justice is *tsedek,* while the word for charity is *tsedaka,* both terms stemming from the same root. A righteous person is known as a *tsadik* (also from the same root), meaning someone who combines justice and charity.

The story is told of a skinflint, known far and wide in the old shtetl for his miserliness. One day he lost his wallet, and at his wife's suggestion posted a notice that anyone finding it and returning it to him would be rewarded generously.

An impoverished man did come upon the wallet and returned it immediately to the owner, and of course waited for the promised reward. The miser, now that he had his wallet back in his possession, pretended that there should have been five hundred rubles and there were now only three hundred. "You are not entitled to any reward," he informed the poor man who had brought him the lost purse.

The pauper turned to the town rabbi, assuring him that he never even considered taking any money out of the wallet, and insisting that the avaricious miser was merely trying to avoid paying him a reward. The rabbi believed the poor man, gave the matter some thought, and then sent for the tightwad to appear before him.

Assuming his judicial tone, the rabbi (who sat as a judge in the town's religious court) asked the miser, "How much was in your lost wallet?" "Five hundred rubles," the tightwad replied. Now the rabbi turned to the elderly pauper who had found the lost purse: "How much was in the wallet that you found?" "Three hundred rubles," the pauper replied.

"Then it is clear—the purse you found does not belong to this man," the rabbi proclaimed. He turned to the miser and ruled, "Give the wallet with the three hundred rubles to this man till the true owner appears."

Tired of Potatoes

The rabbi in the shtetl involved himself in spiritual and religious matters only. He left all material considerations to his wife and to his congregation. Once, after he had adjudicated a dispute between two members of his synagogue, the two men thanked him and then handed him a piece of paper. He glanced at it, turning it over a few times, and then asked, "What is this?"

One of the two men replied, "It's money, Rabbi."

"What's money?" the spiritual leader asked.

"It's something you use to get things with, like food and coal and clothes. What you're holding is ten rubles."

"What shall I do with it?" the rabbi asked.

126

"Give it to your wife," the two men said. "She'll know." The rabbi pondered a little, and then said, "Well, so give me a little more, so she can buy some fish and meat—I'm tired of potatoes."

Ten-Day Suit

A peasant walked into a tailor shop owned by a Jew in a shtetl.

"I need a pair of pants made up," he said. "How long will it take?"

"Ten days."

"Ten days? Why so long? Didn't your God make the whole world in six days—and you need ten days for a pair of pants?"

The tailor picked up a pair of trousers from his rack, and showed the garment to the peasant. "Look at this workmanship," he said. "Now look around the world—see why I need ten days?"

Guess Again

In a small town in Poland before the First World War, a Jewish youngster was on his way to school when a tough-looking Pole stopped him.

"Hey, Moshke," he shouted, "which way to the railroad station?"

The boy paused in his tracks. "How do you know my name is Moshke?" he called out to the Pole.

"I just guessed it."

"So guess your way to the railroad station."

Fair Exchange

Mottel earned his living in the old country by selling pots and pans, traveling constantly from shtetl to shtetl. Practically all of his meals were eaten in restaurants or dining rooms of the small inns in which he stayed. Over a period of time Mottel developed a few ploys, in order to save a few coins.

Once he was in a small restaurant and asked the waitress to bring him two onion rolls. When she placed them on the table, he stopped her and said he was sorry, but he would rather have two bagels instead. She said that was fine, took the rolls away, and brought him two bagels. After Mottel had finished eating the bagels, he rose to leave, but the waitress stood in the doorway and reminded him that he had not paid for the bagels.

"Why should I pay for the bagels?" he asked. "Didn't you get two onion rolls from me in exchange?"

"Yes, but you didn't pay for them."

"Why should I pay for them? I didn't eat them."

Feeding the Horses

In the shtetl, two friends, both in their nineties, are talking. One announces that he received a letter from his grandson in America, and he writes that he had just bought an automobile that has the power of thirty horses.

The second older gentleman thinks hard for a

128

minute and then says: "Really? And where does he get so much hay to feed these horses?"

A Changed Son

Avraham Mandelbaum left his small Polish shtetl while he was still a teenager. Traveling by steerage, he crossed the Atlantic, landed in New York, was taken in to a cousin's Brooklyn apartment, and after some two decades he succeeded in picking himself up by his proverbial bootstraps. Now in his early fifties, he was a prosperous manufacturer of ladies' coats, he had a wife and three children, and had moved to an expensive Park Avenue apartment. He had also shaved off his beard and had gone to court to change his name to Alan Moore.

A few years before the outbreak of World War II he sailed for Europe, eager to see his aging parents before they passed on. When he arrived in his poor hamlet, driven there by a chauffeur in a large English car, his parents were naturally thrilled. When they greeted their son, they were surprised by his appearance.

"What happened to your beard, Avrahama'le?" his mother asked.

"I shaved it off, Mama," he replied. "In America, people don't wear beards. And now people call me Alan, not Avraham."

There was a moment of silence as the elderly parents looked at each other. The father then spoke up: "But you're still circumcised?"

129

Mother's Welfare

In this particular shtetl there lived a young man who was known as the community's atheist. One early Saturday morning his young wife gave birth to their first child. Everything went well but the new father wanted to attach a small, printed quotation from the Book of Psalms above his wife's bed. In the shtetl this was a well-established custom.

He rushed to the home of the town bookseller and asked to buy the good-luck inscription.

"I'm sorry," the bookseller said, "you know today is the Sabbath and I don't open my store on Saturday."

The young father grew irate. "So? Because of your fanaticism you are going to endanger the well-being of a Jewish mother!" he shouted.

A Spa Surprises

A wealthy man in the shtetl went to a spa in Austria, something he had never done before. When he returned home, his fellow congregants asked him what was it like.

"Well, it's like this," he said. "We get up early—like we do for the *selichot* service before the High Holy Days. Then we fast, just like on Yom Kippur. And then we run to the water, just as we do on Rosh Hashanah to cast our sins away at Tashlich."

◆◆◆◆◆◆◆◆◆◆ **8** ◆◆◆◆◆◆◆◆◆◆

Husbands and Wives, and Vice Versa

A man should leave his parents (when he grows up), and marry, the Bible teaches. And the ancient sages of the Talmud, as recorded in the *Ethics of the Fathers* anthology, taught that when a man finds a good wife, he has found goodness. Other rabbis taught that one should not refer to one's wife as such, but consider her one's "home."

In an era when divorce is so widespread and prevalent and easy, it is a pleasure to look at happily married, totally complementary couples and mutter with envy, What is their secret? Perhaps it is common sense, or just luck, or the result of individual personalities that have finally learned to mesh together perfectly.

"Good Snabbath"

Isaac and Ethel had been married for more than fifty years. They were both seventy years old and had lived a full, happy life. Luckily, both enjoyed good health and were reasonably free from financial or other worries.

One day in midwinter, Isaac did not feel quite right, and decided to visit a doctor, something he had not done for many years. A new and youngish physician, the doctor examined Isaac thoroughly and pronounced him "very fit." Isaac however was not satisfied; he still did not feel his old, vigorous self.

He sat in the doctor's office, responding to questions that were being put to him.

"How often do you have sex?" the doctor asked.

"Every day," Isaac replied.

"Every day? But you're a man of seventy. Maybe it's too much, maybe you should cut down."

"Whatever you say, Doctor. I'd just like to feel myself again."

The physician pondered for a few moments. Then he said: "I tell you what—why don't you have sex only on those days of the week that have the letter *n*—like Sunday, Monday, and so on. I think that'll help you feel better."

Isaac agreed to follow the doctor's advice, and went home to tell his wife about the examination and what the doctor had recommended. That day happened to be a Sunday, and so that night the elderly couple had sex. There being an *n* in Monday, the next day the couple had sex again. Tuesday they refrained, and Wednesday they resumed their lovemaking. Thursday, they refrained; Friday, they refrained again. On Saturday, the Jewish Sabbath, known as *shabbes,* they awoke early, planning to attend synagogue services.

Ethel turned to her husband and said, *"Gut Shabbes"* (Good Sabbath). Isaac looked at his wife and replied, *"Gut Shnabbes."* They never made it to synagogue that morning.

May-December Surprise

Fred Levy was past eighty and to all intents and purposes he was in reasonably good health. One day he appeared at his doctor's office for his annual checkup. When the examination was over, Fred confided in his doctor that he was getting married again in a few weeks.

"Congratulations!" Dr. Goldsmith said. "Who's the lucky lady?"

"My secretary, and she's only twenty-three."

For a moment, Levy's physician paused, and then, in his best bedside manner, said:

"Fred, listen to me. You're not a kid anymore. She's a baby, next to you. I have a suggestion for you—why don't you take in a boarder? You know, so that she'll have some company; after all, you're still active in business."

For a few moments, Levy was deep in thought. Then he smiled, thanked his doctor, and said, "You know, that's a very good idea."

More than six months passed and Levy returned to his doctor for a minor ailment.

"How's your wife?" the physician asked his patient.

Levy smiled, looking very proud. "She's pregnant," he said.

"That's great," the doctor said, adding, "And how's the boarder?"

Again Levy smiled. "She's pregnant too," he said.

Obedient

Leo: "Tell me, Mendel, do you ever quarrel with your wife?"

Mendel: "Never. If I ever disagree with her, I issue an order to myself—Silence! And I obey orders."

Wanted: Divorce

A Jewish man came to the rabbi of his synagogue, his eyes red from crying. "Please, Rabbi," he sobbed. "Grant me a divorce. Please!"

"But why? What happened?"

"My wife called me an idiot."

"And in all the years you're married, she never called you that before?"

"Yes, but this time it was different."

"What do you mean?"

"Well, I came home from a long business trip, and I went upstairs to the bedroom, and there I found a strange man with my wife." The man dried his eyes. "I said to her, 'Rachel, what is this?' And she yelled at me and said, 'Idiot! Can't you see?'"

Artistic Taste

Velvel and Max had been close friends for more than a half-century. They had not seen each other for over a year. Max, a widower, had heard that his friend had become widowed too, and was therefore very surprised to run into him on Fifth Avenue, walking together with a strange woman, her arm looped through his.

"Velvel, my old friend!" Max had greeted him. "I want you to meet my new wife. We're only married three weeks. Say hello to Anna!"

Greetings were exchanged, but Velvel could hardly disguise his shock. The woman, he thought to himself, was grotesque. She was not even five feet tall, must have weighed over three hundred pounds, had crossed eyes, wore a wig that was askew, revealing a bald head, and when she spoke her voice was as deep as that of a burly truck driver. When she excused herself to use the facilities of the public library, Max asked his friend, "Well, what do you think? Nice, isn't she?"

Velvel hemmed and hawed, and searched for a kind word to say, but could think of nothing. His eyes remained glued to the sidewalk, averted from his friend. Finally, Max understood that Velvel could not bring himself to say something complimentary about his new wife.

In a burst of anger he yelled at Max: "What's the matter? You don't like Picasso?"

Heavenly Happy

The Cohens, a happily married couple for more than forty years, were killed in an automobile accident. Mourning was widespread among their many friends and family members, and in the suburban community where they had lived for three decades.

The scene now shifts. Lillian and Maurice Cohen are doing their thing in heaven. In their case, doing their thing means they are playing golf in the morning, enjoying a beautiful luncheon catered by pleasant waitresses, delighting in the tennis courts all afternoon, dining in style for dinner, and roaring with pleasure at a superb theatrical performance in the evening.

This pleasure-filled regimen went on for several months, and neither Lillian nor Maurice ceased to wonder at their good fortune. One day, as the couple was returning home from their daily tennis game, Maurice suddenly turned angry. He grabbed his wife's arm roughly, his usually benign expression now twisted and raging.

"You and your damned oatmeal!" he shouted at her. "Imagine, we could have been here five years ago!"

Marital Woes

Rabbi Stern was a relatively new official in the synagogue. When he was hired by the board, he had proudly announced that he had completed a course in family counseling at the rabbinical seminary, and was anxious and ready to offer his services to the congregation.

Soon after, a young woman member was seated in the rabbi's study. Her eyes were puffy, and she found it difficult to refrain from crying. "This man, Rabbi," she started. "All he wants is to kiss me— kiss, kiss, and more kiss. How can I stop him?"

"Look here, put your foot down. Be firm," the rabbi advised. "Tell him no, and if he persists, order him to leave."

Two weeks later the young woman was back in the rabbi's study. She still looked forlorn and upset. "I don't know how to tell you, Rabbi," she said. "All he wants is to touch me—his hands are all over me. I don't know what to do!"

The rabbi became furious. "That scoundrel!" he shouted. "Tell him to keep his hands to himself. He is not to touch you or kiss you, and if he insists, you call the police. If necessary, I'll come over and throw the bum out. This is disgraceful!"

Two more weeks passed, and again the young woman congregant was in the rabbi's study. She sat demurely, her hands folded over a soaked handkerchief. "Rabbi, since I saw you, all he wants is to sleep with me," she said.

"That arrogant cad!" the rabbi exclaimed.

"Of course I said no—no kissing, no touching, and no sleeping with me," the young woman continued. "And now, now he wants a divorce."

A Child Is Named

A young couple was blessed with a newborn infant, a little boy who came into the world looking and

137

acting like a healthy and happy child. The young parents, however, found that there was a fly in the proverbial ointment. The mother wanted to name the child for her deceased father, who had been a respected rabbi and scholar, while the husband wished to name his son for his father, who had been a petty thief who had even served time in jail. The parents could not settle the argument and decided to take it to the local *beit-din,* the religious court, for arbitration.

The presiding judge was a rabbi known for his insight and understanding. He listened while each parent pleaded for the son to be named for the respective, departed father. Finally, he asked the mother, "What was your father's Hebrew name?" "Mordecai," she replied. Then he asked the father the same question and was surprised to learn that his father too had been called Mordecai.

The rabbi sat back, closed his eyes, stroked his beard a little. And then he offered the couple his decision. "Look, name the child Mordecai," he said. "If he grows up and becomes a rabbi and scholar, then you'll know he was named for the mother's father, and if, God forbid, he becomes a thief, then it will be for the father's father."

Special Prayer

An elderly shtetl woman approached the rabbi.

"Tell me, Rabbi," she asked, "is there a special prayer against a bad husband—like one against a bad wife?"

The rabbi sighed. "No, there's no such prayer— in both cases, prayers don't help."

9

Parents and Children— Oy!

There is a word that is used frequently in Hebrew and Yiddish that is nonexistent in any other language. It is almost untranslatable. The word is *na'ches,* with the *ch* pronounced the German guttural way, as in *ach.*

Na'ches is a term reserved solely for parental joy and pleasure. No one else but one's children can either give or—God forbid—withhold na'ches. People wish one another *gezunt* (health), *na'ches,* and *parnasah* (a livelihood). In fact, as one wit notes, while the letters GNP mean gross national product in referring to a nation's output, in one's personal life it refers to *gezunt, na'ches,* and *parnasah.*

Journey to a Guru

Molly Moskowitz was a wealthy widow. She had one son, Sheldon, whom she had not seen in nearly

139

four years. One day she visited a travel agency that specialized in trips to India, and asked to join a group that was getting ready for a difficult journey to a remote corner of the Himalayas.

The travel agent tried to discourage her, explaining that there was considerable hardship in reaching the distant destination. "Part of the way you have to ride on a mountain donkey, and part of the way, it's uphill, in snow and ice," the agent said. But Mrs. Moskowitz could not be dissuaded.

She insisted on signing up, and in the course of a few weeks she had flown to India, journeyed by bus to a city at the Himalayan foothills, walked up part of one mountain, and had ridden in snow and sleet on a donkey up another steep incline. Finally, at the end of three weeks the party of travelers arrived at the Shangri-La-like retreat high up in the tallest mountains on earth. For many of her fellow travelers, Mrs. Moskowitz had learned, this was a spiritual journey, since many of them hoped to meet and come under the spell of a guru leader whose fame had spread around the world.

Mrs. Moskowitz was shown to a small alcove in the spacious building occupied by the guru and his followers and visitors. Although she was tired from her arduous trek, she did not bother to unpack or rest. She proceeded directly to the main room of the edifice in which she was located, where she had been told she would find the group's guru.

In the middle of the room that she entered she could see more than one hundred people. Most of them seemed to be wearing a long, gownlike garment. Some of the people were chanting softly, while others were tinkling small bells. Somewhat elevated on a gold-colored stool sat the guru, a youngish man who looked years older because of his scraggly beard and unkempt hair.

Mrs. Moskowitz looked around for a moment, taking it all in. Then, taking a deep breath, she marched through the crowd of worshipers and presented herself directly in front of the guru, whose eyes were closed in concentration, and who was swaying to and fro, and chanting. Mrs. Moskowitz's hands moved up to her hips; her face took on a look of annoyance and frustration; she bent forward toward the guru, and in a loud, strong voice addressed him, so that everyone could hear:

"Sheldon Moskowitz, enough already! It's time to go home!"

First Date

Rabbi and Mrs. Gershman were nervous. Their daughter, Rebecca, a beautiful eighteen-year-old freshman at Yeshiva University's Stern College, was getting ready for her first date. She had been reared in a strictly Orthodox home, had attended all-girl schools, and had never really gotten to know many young men. Her parents knew that the young man who was coming to call for her was the brother of Rebecca's classmate and came from a respectable family. Nevertheless, since she was their only daughter, and this was in the latter years of the twentieth century, they were nervous.

At the appointed hour, the young man arrived and made an excellent impression on Rebecca and on her parents. They left the family home around seven in the evening, and just before midnight Rebecca came home, looking happy. Her mother had gone to bed, but the rabbi was still up.

"Did you have a nice evening?" Rebecca's father asked his daughter.

"Very nice, in fact very, very nice," she said. "He's an interesting person."

The father cleared his throat; for a moment he seemed embarrassed. "I assume," he said, "that he behaved like a perfect gentleman?"

Rebecca smiled. "Well, there's a phrase from the Bible that does come to mind, when you ask me that. Remember the line? 'The voice is the voice of Jacob, but the hands are the hands of Esau.' "

Not Her Type

Mr. and Mrs. Abraham Goodman were members of a suburban synagogue. They were active members, whose only child, Julia, had graduated from the synagogue's religious school with honors, and had even gone on to the regional Jewish religious high school for a few years.

The hopes that they had for her had fizzled. She had dropped out of college, waited on tables in San Francisco, dated non-Jewish young men, and whenever she was introduced to a possible marital partner, she fumed and made a scene. Now she was back home, close to thirty-two years of age, the mother of three small children, unmarried, and content to stay home all day and let her parents support her and her children.

Unable to communicate meaningfully with their

daughter, the Goodman couple went to their rabbi for help and counseling. He listened carefully as they recited the story of their daughter's life, and offered to talk to her, hoping it would help.

A few days later, the rabbi was in the living room of the Goodmans' home, seated opposite Julia. The children were outside, playing, watched over by their grandparents.

The rabbi plunged right in. "Julia," he said, "I'm trying to be helpful, believe me. Tell me, the children—are they all from one man, or three different men?"

"Oh, Rabbi, what do you take me for?" Julia said. "Of course from one man."

The rabbi felt encouraged. "Then why"—he smiled as he spoke—"why don't you get married to him?"

"I couldn't do that, Rabbi," Julia said. "He's just not my type."

A Daughter Marries

Mrs. Shapiro and Mrs. Greenberg had been close friends for nearly fifty years. Both women were widowed and looked forward to their weekly lunches avidly.

After the waiter took their orders, Mrs. Shapiro turned to her friend. "I have nice news, Marilyn," she said. "My daughter is getting married again."

"Mazel tov!" her friend responded, bussing her friend on the cheek.

"Who is she marrying?"

"Dr. Lester Gottheil, the cardiologist!"

Mrs. Greenberg was overwhelmed. Dr. Gottheil was considered the most eligible bachelor in town. He was a renowned medical researcher.

"That's wonderful," Mrs. Greenberg said. "Let me think—wasn't your daughter once married to Harold Braverman, the famous lawyer?"

"Yes, she certainly was," Mrs. Shapiro replied. "And before that, she was married to Nathan Winkler, the investment banker."

Mrs. Greenberg pondered what her friend had said, digesting the information carefully. Finally she spoke, her face beaming.

"Imagine!" she said. "So much *naches* from one child!"

A Good Son

Mrs. Lipshutz was confiding in her friend, Mrs. Lieberman, about her son's trials and tribulations. "He goes to the psychiatrist," she said. "Every day almost, and they talk and talk."

"About what?" Mrs. Lieberman asked.

"I don't know exactly, but my son said the doctor told him he has an Oedipus complex. What it is, I don't know."

"Ah, Oedipus, shmoedipus—so long as he loves his mama!"

"Have a Good Time!"

Arnold was the son of a prosperous set of parents. His parents—according to all their friends and rela-

144

tives—spoiled him rotten. An only child, he was given piano and tennis lessons, sent to the fanciest summer camps, taken to Broadway shows and restaurants, clad in the newest styles, and provided at an early age with an expensive stereo system, personal computer, and at age eighteen, a shiny red Corvette.

Nevertheless, he was not a happy or well-adjusted youth, and barely managed to be accepted at an upstate New York branch of the state's network of colleges, although his parents had their eyes on Harvard or Yale. After two years at college, Arnold was still looking—for himself. He had earlier announced that he did not want to go into his father's successful real estate business, nor did he have any desire to study law, medicine, accounting, computers, or any other subject.

His grades hovered between D's and failures; his usual manner toward his parents was sullen and abrasive. Over the years his hair had grown longer, his speech less comprehensible as he ingested a whole culture of new language that was part of the drug-related culture, and his capacity to infuriate his parents seemed boundless.

One evening Arnold was at home waiting for his beloved car to be repaired after a sixteen-wheel truck had rear-ended it. His mother was at her usual Tuesday evening mah-jongg game and his father was watching a televised baseball game.

Arnold cleared his throat. "Pop, can I borrow your car tonight?" he asked.

His indulgent father smiled, apparently glad that his son even talked to him. "Sure," he said, tossing his car keys across the room.

Arnold continued: "Eh, listen, you know, I'm broke. Can you lend me fifty?" His father smiled, reaching for his wallet. "Sure," he said, and handed over two twenties and a ten to his son.

Arnold paused, and then continued. "Listen, Pop. I noticed you just got yourself a nifty-looking sports jacket, you know, the blue velvet. Think I could borrow it tonight?"

Again his father smiled. "Sure thing," he said, "you know where it is—take it."

Arnold nodded, headed for his father's closet, slipped the jacket on, put the newly acquired fifty dollars into his pocket, and holding on to his father's car keys, walked through the den toward the garage door. His father's voice stopped him.

"Hey, Arnie," his father called out. "You look terrific."

Arnold responded with an almost imperceptible nod.

"Have a good time, son," his father called out.

Arnold stopped in midstride, swung around, his face now contorted in an angry expression. "Don't you ever tell me what to do!" he shouted.

And then went out for the evening.

Proud Mother

Mrs. Goldman was bragging about her child to her friend, Mrs. Levy. "Susan and her husband just bought a beautiful new house," she reports. "And

Cindy's husband just gave her a sable coat, after she gave birth to their third child."

"That's wonderful. Tell me, what about Jack?"

"Well, you know he goes three times a week to talk to his doctor," she said. "A special doctor, for the mind, a psychiatrist. And guess what he talks about all the time. Me!"

◆◆◆◆◆◆◆◆◆ 10 ◆◆◆◆◆◆◆◆◆

Doctors Are Healers—
Mostly!

Maimonides, one of the greatest Jewish philosophers and scholars of Judaism of all time, was also a physician. The profession of medicine has drawn Jews for many years, and indeed there has developed in recent years a kind of mystique about Jewish doctors; i.e., they have a special talent for curing and healing the sick.

Jewish physicians and medical researchers who add to mankind's conquest of disease (like Jonas Salk and polio) become major sources of pride to the Jewish community. This does not mean, however, that lots of Jewish patients do not approach their doctors with a certain sense of skepticism.

Where to Send the Bill

Sidney Abramowitz, a cantankeous old man, was walking down the street in Chicago when he was hit and badly injured by a truck. He was rushed to a nearby Catholic hospital, where his injuries were attended to, and later he was taken to a room where it was hoped he would recover in the course of the next week. "Who'll be responsible for the bill?" the nun in charge asked him.

The old man snorted. "Listen, I have no money. My only living relative is my sister, but she converted and became a nun and an old maid."

The nun tried to hide her annoyance. "We are not old maids, sir," she said. "We are married to Jesus."

"In that case," Abramowitz said, "send the bill to my brother-in-law."

Patient Likes to Talk

A patient in a psychiatrist's office explains his problem: "Doctor, lately I find that I'm talking to myself," he says.

"It's nothing, lots of people do that."

"But, Doctor, you don't know what a *nudnik* I can be!"

How to Listen

Two Jewish psychiatrists maintain offices in the same Fifth Avenue office building. One evening, close to 9 P.M., they meet in the lobby after a long day. The younger of the two men, Dr. Rosenbloom, turns to his colleague, Dr. Frishman, and asks: "Max, just between the two of us, how come when you leave here after a whole day of listening to your patients, you look perfectly fresh and relaxed, like it's the morning, not the evening. Me—look at me—I feel drained and exhausted. Just listening to these poor devils saps all of my strength."

The older doctor smiled, patted his colleague, and said: "So, who listens?"

Jews Sank the Titanic?

Two physicians have been friends for many years. One is Jewish and the other Chinese. One evening, the two of them are relaxing in a hotel bar, after spending the last few days listening to reports of new, advanced methods of medical treatment. They are both nursing beers.

"You know, Joe," the Jewish doctor says to his friend and colleague, Dr. Joseph Chang, "we've been friends for thirty years—and I think that's remarkable, after what you people did at Pearl Harbor."

"Pearl Harbor?" the Chinese physician exclaims. "Abe, I'm Chinese, not Japanese."

"Oh, what's the difference—Chinese, Japanese, Korean, Vietnamese, it's all the same to me."

Dr. Chang hesitates, and then says: "You know, you're right. After all, we have been good friends all these years, even though sometimes it's hard for me to forget what you people did to the Titanic."

"The Titanic? What are you talking about? That was an iceberg."

"Well, you know, it's all the same to me—
Goldberg, Rosenberg, iceberg."

Happy Wife

An elderly Jew is lying in the hospital bed, deathly
ill. Standing alongside are his doctor and his wife.

"Please, Doctor," the wife cries out. "How long
will he have to suffer like this?"

At this point the sick old man opens his eyes,
stares at his wife, and shouts, "Get away from
here, you harridan, you shrew!"

The wife turns to the doctor, smiling. "Oh,
Doctor," she exults, "he's getting better—he recognized me!"

Take Two Teaspoons

Pinchas the pickpocket was ailing and was now
hospitalized. The doctor came to examine him,
and after checking him out thoroughly, recommended that Pinchas take a prescribed medicine.
"Take a teaspoon every two hours," the doctor
admonished.

"What kind of spoon, silver or tin?" Pinchas
asked.

"It doesn't matter, it can be plain tin."

"I don't think it'll work, Doctor. I once took a
whole tray full of silver spoons, and look, I'm still
sick."

No Doctor's Fee

A miserly physician in the shtetl was known to be more concerned about his fees than about his patients. Once, a poor tailor in town called him in to treat his sick wife. The doctor arrived at the man's modest home, and saw immediately that it would be difficult to earn a big fee. He told the tailor that his wife was very ill, the chances of her recovery were slim, and the prospects for his being properly paid for his time and services were equally dim.

The tailor, his eyes filled with tears, pleaded with the doctor. "I'll pay you," he said, "whether you cure her or kill her, I'll pay you." The doctor nodded his agreement, and treated the sick woman for several days, but nothing availed. She died during the night, and the next day the doctor sent the tailor a bill for one thousand rubles.

The tailor said the sum was exorbitant, and refused to pay. The doctor then summoned the tailor to the religious tribunal in town, where both men presented their respective versions of what had happened.

The presiding rabbi turned to the doctor:

"Did you cure her?"

"No, Rabbi, she was too sick."

"Did you kill her?"

"Of course not!"

"Then you're not entitled to a single ruble. Case closed."

Second Opinion

David Halpern goes to the doctor, is examined thoroughly, and is told by the physician, "You're a sick man."

Halpern retorts: "I want another opinion."

"All right," the doctor says, "you're also homely."

Medical Advice

Abraham Greenberg went to the doctor for a checkup, only because his wife had threatened to divorce him if he didn't. He hated doctors and had not been to see one for more than twenty-five years.

Dr. Fried examined Greenberg thoroughly, and then questioned him:

"Do you drink?"

"Yup, a pint a day."

"How about smoking?"

"Two, maybe three packs a day."

"Well, listen, my friend, I'm going to give you some advice—you had better stop drinking entirely and cut out smoking altogether. That's my advice—otherwise, you're a doomed man."

The doctor paused. "Please pay my secretary on your way out—that'll be fifty dollars for my advice."

Greenberg rose from the examining table. "Who's taking it?" he asked, as he left the office.

A New Disease?

An elderly Jewish woman lived alone in an apartment house located on Manhattan's Riverside Drive. She had few friends and few people came to see her. One day she awoke feeling ill, and remembered that one of the new neighbors, a fine-looking gentleman who wore a neat goatee, had been referred to by another neighbor as "Doctor." She decided to visit him; perhaps he could diagnose her illness and prescribe some medicine.

She knocked on the man's door. He recognized her, and asked her in.

"What can I do for you?" he asked.

"Well, Doctor, I got up this morning, and my chest hurts and I was wondering if you could help me."

"I'm awfully sorry, I'm not that kind of doctor—I'm a doctor of philosophy."

She looked at him, without comprehension.

"Tell me, Doctor," she said. "What kind of disease is philosophy?"

Making a Living

Mrs. Cohen, aged seventy-five, had never seen a gynecologist. And now, at her daughter's urging, she found herself in a young gynecologist's office. She first answered some questions put to her by Dr. Morse's nurse, and then was asked to step behind a screen and remove her clothes so that the doctor could examine her.

155

Cautiously she stepped away from the screen, wearing a loose gown. Dr. Morse approached, and Mrs. Cohen remonstrated with him: "Tell me, Doctor, your mother knows that from this you make a living?"

Gentile Nurse

Overheard in a ladies' lounge in a fancy New York restaurant: Two attractive young Jewish women are talking softly, and one confides in the other, "On Saturday, I pretended I was a Gentile nurse."

"What do you mean, a Gentile nurse?"

"I slept with a Jewish doctor."

11

Festive Touches on Special Days

Jews celebrate the national holidays of their countries of residence. In the United States, American Jews hang out flags on the Fourth of July, sit down to a turkey dinner on Thanksgiving Day, remember the fallen on Memorial Day, vacation on Labor Day, and usher in the New Year with a bang on the night of December 31. And in addition, they celebrate Purim, Passover, Shavuot, Sukkot, Simchat Torah, Chanukah, Tu B'Shvat, Israel Independence Day—and of course the very special High Holy Days, Rosh Hashanah and Yom Kippur.

Thus, if one sees a Jewish family busily flitting from one festive occasion to another, there is a good reason.

Better Odds

Benjamin Golub owned a pet shop in the Long Island suburban town he had resided in for more than thirty years. One year, on the eve of Rosh Hashanah, he brought a parrot to the synagogue. The usher tried to stop him from bringing the bird into the sanctuary. Golub argued angrily: "Listen, this parrot can pray better than anyone in this temple!" The usher snickered. "Oh, yeah," he said, "my five dollars to your one says he can't even open his mouth and utter one Hebrew word."

Golub turned to his pet parrot. "Okay, kid, you show them," he said. "Recite the whole *Shma* prayer."

The parrot remained mute and motionless, despite Golub's repeated urging. Disgusted and somewhat humiliated, he took the bird and went home, skipping services.

The parrot was placed in his cage, while Golub admonished him for refusing to pray and show his knowledge of Hebrew. The parrot chortled, and then spoke, "Yeah, yeah, but think of the odds you can get on Yom Kippur!"

Dowry Help

A friend calls on an old acquaintance, on Yom Kippur.

"How about a cup of coffee and a Danish?" the guest says.

"On Yom Kippur? You know every Jew fasts today."

"Well, I want a cup of coffee because I want to earn a mitzvah, a good deed."

"What are you talking about?"

"Last week, I heard you say that you wished

your daughter's dowry could be as big as the number of Jews who don't fast on Yom Kippur—so if I eat something today, I'll be adding to her dowry."

Matzoh Won't Work

On Passover eve the village's richest inhabitant invited a poor traveler home for the seder. It was pretty obvious that the poor fellow had not had a decent meal for a long time. When the hostess served him a portion of gefilte fish, he devoured it in two bites. Then he spoke:

"You know, I'm going to have another piece of this delicious fish, in honor of Passover, which after all celebrates the splitting of the sea when the Israelites walked right through, and fish of course come from the sea."

Then he took two more pieces of fish, declaring that "Passover is a holiday that honors Moses and Aaron, and that's why I'm eating two more portions of fish, in their honor."

The host now called out to his wife. "Manya, take away the fish," he said, "before our guest decides to honor each one of the six hundred thousand Jews who fled Egypt at the time of the Exodus."

Haman's Daughter

Two old Jewish friends are in synagogue to attend the annual Purim festival service. This is the one Jewish holiday when Jews are encouraged to drink and be merry, and when it is permissible to become so intoxicated that one cannot distinguish between Mordecai (the hero of Purim) and Haman (the villain).

One of the two friends, Isaac, comments to his old pal, Louis:

"You know, it's Purim, and we remember that Haman and all his ten sons were hanged for trying to exterminate all the Jews in ancient Persia."

"So?"

"I'll bet you didn't know Haman also had a daughter."

"Really? I never knew that. Did they hang her too?"

"No—she became my wife."

Neighborly Example

A simpleton decided one year that he wished to conduct a Passover seder, but he had no idea what to do. He turned to his wife, whose name was Deborah, and told her to get dressed, walk across the lawn, and peek into the house next door where the Levines lived.

"You'll see what they do," he said, "and then come back and tell me, and we'll do exactly the same thing."

Deborah got dressed, left the house, and when she returned in ten minutes, she began immediately to batter her husband with a rolling pin.

"What are you doing?" her husband yelled at her. "Are you crazy?"

"You said I should do what the Levines are

doing," Deborah said. "Mrs. Levine is hitting Mr. Levine, just like I was doing to you."

Purim Question

It is customary to have a festive meal on the occasion of the Purim holiday. This is often called the Purim *se'udah*.

One day, the rabbi and his wife were invited to the Purim se'udah at the home of their congregants, Joseph and Frieda Gordon. The Gordons' son, Michael, who was fourteen, was known as a *nudnik,* a kind of pest who seemed to enjoy posing inane questions.

At the table Michael turned to the rabbi and asked: "Rabbi, tell me, when the Book of Esther tells how Haman's ten sons were hanged, it says that Vaizatha was the last one to be executed. Why? Why not first?"

The rabbi replied at once: "Vaizatha was known as a fool, you see. And it is well known, 'Don't start in with a fool.' "

Half Ready

It is a few days before Passover. The head of one poor Jewish family in Brooklyn is accosted by a social worker from a Jewish welfare agency. "Are you all set for Passover?" the young woman asks.

"Well, I'm half set."

"Half? What do you mean, half?"

"I've thrown out the *chametz,* all the leavened

161

food—now all I need is to obtain the matzohs, wine, and everything else we need for the Passover holiday.''

Divine Equality

An impoverished Jewish man met a very wealthy shtetl Jew just prior to the Passover holiday. The rich man asked the poor man, ''Well, my friend, how goes it with you? Any news?''

''I tell you, yes, I finally figured out that the good Lord is just and practices equality. Look, it's almost Passover, and God has given you four things for the holiday—matzohs, fish, meat, and wine. And for paupers like me, He has also sent us four things—the darkness of Egypt, bitter herbs, the ten plagues, and a mouth that needs feeding.''

12

Matchmakers: Gone with the Wind?

When a couple gets married nowadays, it turns out that they met in college or at work, or were introduced by a mutual friend, or they spotted each other in synagogue or at a dance or a resort hotel.

But not so very long ago, there existed in Europe the institution of the matchmaker, the *shadchan,* whose job it was to ferret out eligible and unmarried people and bring them together in what was hoped would be a state of lifelong wedded bliss.

To some extent there are still some matchmakers active in the United States and Israel, who work at this odd calling as a vocation. And there are also thousands of volunteer matchmakers, well-meaning friends and relatives, who can't wait to exclaim: "Have I got a girl (or fellow) for you to meet!" And lots of times, to everyone's surprise, it works out fine.

A Matchmaker Fails

In the old country, the *shadchan* was an established community institution. He or she would, for a fee that depended on the wealth of the parents involved, seek to introduce an unmarried young man to a suitable, unmarried young woman. In the Jewish community in those days, and nowadays too, two biblical commands still resound loud and clear. One says: "It is not good for a man to be alone" and the other declares "Be fruitful and multiply." So the *shadchan* knew he had solid religious grounds for his vocation. Of course by the nature of his or her calling, the *shadchan* was often the butt of derisive jokes.

One day, for example, a young man was brought to the home of a family whose unmarried daughter was a serious prospect for a groom. The table was laid out beautifully, the parents were extremely solicitous, but the groom-to-be was shocked by the girl's appearance. To say she was plain was a kindness.

After the meal, the young man grabbed the *shadchan* outside the family's hearing. "What's wrong with you?" he shouted at the matchmaker. "She's impossible to look at, she can't say two words, and she doesn't have a ruble! This you call a match for me!" The prospective bridegroom lowered his voice. "I shouldn't talk so loud, I don't have to hurt her feelings also."

"Don't worry," the matchmaker chimed in, "she's deaf."

One Fault Only

The town matchmaker was trying to impress an eligible young woman with a prospective young man.

"I tell you, he's just a marvelous fellow," he said. "He has every conceivable good trait—really, a wonderful young man!"

The young woman nodded, and certainly seemed to be interested.

The matchmaker continued: "There is only one flaw—he stammers."

The prospective bride mulled it over. "Does he always stammer?" she asked.

"No, no, only when he talks."

A Dubious Groom

One day the matchmaker is heard asking a young man what he thought of the family with whom he had dined the night before, and whose only daughter was an eligible bride.

The young man hesitated. "Well, it was a very nice dinner," he said. "The girl's nice too, I have to admit. The only thing is—are you sure those people are really wealthy? How do you know they didn't borrow all that fancy silverware, just to make an impression?"

"Are you crazy? Who would lend silverware to that pack of thieves?"

Hyperbolic Aide

The town *shadchan* was no longer a young man, and he found it hard to get around to visit prospective clients. He hired a healthy adolescent to drive him, and to act as his one-man claque. The *shadchan* instructed him to add hyperbole and exaggeration to everything he said to a potential client.

"If I say the family is rich," the matchmaker told his young aide, "you jump in and say, 'They're practically millionaires.' All right?"

One day the two men were visiting the parents of a young man who had expressed interest in getting married. The *shadchan* was lauding a particular young woman, the daughter of the town grocer.

"She comes from a marvelous family," he said.

"Descendants of King David," the young assistant chimed in.

"She also happens to be very pretty," the matchmaker added.

"What do you mean pretty?" the assistant interpolated. "A beauty!"

"Well, I have to tell you one small negative thing," the *shadchan* said. "She has a wart on her back."

"A wart?" the assistant echoed. "It's as big as a hump!"

No Time to Look

A matchmaker was trying to arrange a marriage between a student in the local yeshiva and the daughter of a rich man. Although the young lady in question came from a good family and was generally known to possess a good character, and to have had a generous education, she was, unfortunately, rather plain. Indeed, she was more than plain—she was homely.

The yeshiva student, a fine young man in his early twenties, had been invited for dinner at the girl's family home. It was now the day after, and he was reporting to the matchmaker.

"Look, the family is nice, I know they're ready to finance my continuing studies, and she's a fine person—but frankly, I'm afraid I'll be miserable all my life. I just can't look at her, she's so ugly."

The matchmaker retorted angrily: "What are you saying? Listen, you are in the yeshiva all day, studying. Are you looking at her? No! You go home, she serves you dinner, you don't look at her, you eat your meal. And then you go to bed, it's dark, you don't look at her. And in the morning, you rise early, you put on your tefillin, and you hold your prayer book, your eyes are closed in devotion, and you pray. And you don't look at her. And then, after you're married, please God, you'll have many children, it's the Sabbath, you've just enjoyed a wonderful meal, your wife is cleaning up, and you take the children for a walk, and you look at them, and at nature, at the trees and flowers. So, tell me, I admit she's ugly, but when will you ever look at her?"

Taste in Art

A young man, a prospective groom, confronts the *shadchan* who had arranged a date with a young woman, who was seeking to get married. The young man was furious.

"What are you, nuts?" he shouted at the matchmaker. "The girl's positively ugly! Did you see the shape of her nose?"

"Well, you either like Picasso or you don't."

13

In the Animal Kingdom

The Bible teaches that a "righteous man regards the life of his beast." And the Talmud instructs Jews to refrain from eating "before you have fed your animal." Elsewhere the Talmud states: "To relieve an animal of pain or danger (with reference to Sabbath observance) is a biblical law, superseding any rabbinic ordinance."

Although this is not too well known, Judaism has always taught that people must be especially compassionate to members of the animal kingdom. The laws of ritual slaughter focus on minimizing pain for an animal that is about to be killed for food.

One wonders if there is a pet shop in the ultra-orthodox Boro Park section of Brooklyn, where the parrots speak Yiddish and cite Talmudic passages.

Not Her Dog

A widowed New Yorker, Mrs. Anna Rothstein, flew on El Al to Israel; she was a frequent visitor and the crewmembers went out of their way to make her comfortable. As the giant jumbo prepared for takeoff, she summoned one of the stewardesses. "Miriam," she said to her, "when you get a chance, ask about my dog, how everything is back there in cargo—I'm taking him to Israel with me."

The plane was now cruising across the ocean; everything seemed to be shipshape, and Miriam now had a chance to talk to the chief steward. She asked about Mrs. Rothstein's dog, and was visibly shaken when she saw him blanch.

"Oy! Oy vay!" he said to her. "We left it in New York, I remember seeing the carrying case, it was marked, and it was supposed to be put on board, and now I realize we never did. She'll kill us!"

The problem was presented to the captain, who made a suggestion. He asked Miriam to chat with Mrs. Rothstein and find out what kind of dog Mrs. Rothstein had. He would then radio ahead and ask El Al to scour all the pet shops, find a perfect match, and when they would land, "she'll never know the difference."

Some nine hours later the plane is now on the tarmac in Israel. Everyone is happy to have had a pleasant journey, and Mrs. Rothstein makes her way off the plane. Miriam the stewardess approaches her, a small fox terrier in her arms. "Here is your dog, Mrs. Rothstein," she says. "It looks like he had a good trip."

The American visitor grabs the nearest handrail; she looks very agitated. "That is not my dog," she replies. "My dog died a week ago and I was bringing him here for burial."

A Cantorial Creature

The idea of talking animals is not uniquely Jewish, although the Bible records one of the earliest such phenomena—the story of Balaam and his talkative donkey.

Rabbis like to tell the story of a congregation whose cantor took ill just before the awesome, somber holiday of Yom Kippur when the entire congregation spends the whole day in prayer and fasting, hoping for a new, good year, and contemplating the events of the year that has just passed.

Anyway, in this particular synagogue the cantor was out of commission and no one in the congregation felt capable of leading the service on Yom Kippur, which has a distinct, traditional liturgy. Things looked bleak until one congregant, Mr. Feldstein, spoke up.

"My dog can lead the service," he said.

The congregation thought for a moment that Feldstein had completely lost his marbles. Voices were raised, some people scoffed, others laughed, and finally somebody suggested that they give the dog a try. After all, he argued, what would they have to lose?

The dog was brought forward to the *bimah,* the raised platform facing the congregation. A *tallit,* a prayer shawl, was placed on the dog, and then quite incredibly the dog began to sing the service—his voice was beautiful, the melody was the centuries-old, traditional song that almost everyone remembered from one Yom Kippur to the next, and soon everyone in the congregation forgot that the cantor who was leading the service was a four-legged animal. Finally, at the end of the day, when the blast of the ram's horn—the *shofar*—announced the end of Yom Kippur and the end of the period of fasting, congregants rushed over to the dog's owner, Mr. Feldstein, and congratulated him. "Your dog is fantastic!" people shouted in unison. "He should be a full-time cantor! He's wonderful!"

Feldstein accepted the compliments gratefully, patting the dog, which was still wearing a prayer shawl, and upon whose head there still rested a small yarmulke.

Finally, the rabbi approached Feldstein. "It's amazing, absolutely amazing," he said to his congregant. "Really, why don't you get him to become a full-time cantor?"

Feldstein sighed. "Rabbi, you talk to him," he said, nodding toward the dog. "He wants to be a doctor!"

Man or Mouse

Morris spotted his friend Sam walking disconsolately along the beach in Miami. "Why do you look so sad?" Sam asked.

"Why? I'll tell you why. I'm trying to figure out what kind of an animal I am."

"What are you talking about?"

"Look—the king of the beasts is the lion, so the bear is afraid of him. A wolf is afraid of the bear, and a mouse is afraid of a cat. Now, what kind of animal am I? My wife is afraid of a mouse—and I'm afraid of my wife!"

Elephantine Bargain

Chaim and Mordecai had been friends for years. Both men were now retired, making do on their Social Security checks and modest union pensions. Chaim had a vivid imagination, and sometimes his fantasies led him astray. Mordecai was much more conservative and set in his ways.

They met in the small park near their respective one-room apartments in Brooklyn, and Chaim said: "Have I got a deal for you! Listen, I can get you an elephant, a trained, peaceful elephant, for only five hundred dollars! What a pet he'll make! And it's no bother to take care of him."

"Are you crazy, completely *meshugga*?" Mordecai responded. "An elephant in my one-room apartment! You must be out of your mind. Besides, it would cost a fortune just to feed him."

Chaim waxed enthusiastic. "No, no, he eats very little, really, I checked up on him," he said. For the next half-hour he continued to extol the elephant he wanted his friend to buy, but it was obvious he had met a solid rejection. Finally, his face lit up and Chaim said:

"Look, Mordecai, you and I have been good friends for a long, long time. I hear your objections, about feeding the elephant and about the fact that

173

you only have one room. I think the real reason you don't want him is because of the money. All right, maybe you're right, for an old friend like you I'm making a special deal—two elephants for six hundred dollars! Take it or leave it."

Mordecai jumped to his feet, grabbed his friend's hand, and pumped it hard, repeating over and over again gleefully, "Now you're talking!"

Feline Tragedy

A Jewish tourist from the United States was driving his rented car in a quiet, residential area of Tel Aviv. He was checking the house numbers, on the lookout for the house of a distant relative he had promised his parents he would look up. For one moment his eyes were off the road; a slow-moving gray cat tried to cross the road, and the inevitable happened—the cat was killed instantly. The driver stopped immediately, stared at the dead animal in the road, and was obviously very upset.

From a nearby house, an elderly man appeared, walking with a cane. The driver, who knew no Hebrew and suspected that the older man did not understand English, spoke in elementary Yiddish.

"This, your cat, sir?" he said.

The old man nodded, his face a mask of sadness. The young American continued:

"I am very, very sorry. Accident. Is there anything I can do?"

The old man shifted his gaze from the cat that lay sprawled in the road, and now peered at the young American tourist. He said: *"Du kenst cha'pen meizlech?"* (Can you catch mice?)

14

Uniquely Individual

The fact that "people are funny" has been hammered into most people's subconscious minds for many years. And then, as you grow older and your circle of friends and acquaintances expands, you realize that it's true—people *are* funny—and strange, ridiculous, unique, inexplicable, unpredictable, and sometimes awesome. And if you regard them through humorous eyes, and gentle philosophy, they're really funny—and then some!

Shul for Golf

Abe Friedman retired early from his business and devoted himself to golf. He loved the game and could be seen out on the links at an early hour almost daily. He took lessons, he practiced driving and putting, he observed professional players carefully, and yet he felt he did not play a good game.

One morning he was concentrating on his game when he noticed an odd-looking golfer not far away. The man wore a large yarmulke and his full beard was speckled with gray and red. And every time he hit the ball, he got a hole in one. Abe watched with growing disbelief and rising envy. Finally he approached the unusual golfer.

"Excuse me," he said. "I have never seen such fantastic playing. How do you do it?"

The bearded golfer smiled enigmatically. "Are you Jewish?" he asked Abe.

"Yes, I am, but what's that got to do with it? I'm talking about your golf. You're unbelievable."

"Listen, my friend," the bearded golfer continued. "If you will attend synagogue services daily for a whole month, and if you will eat only kosher food for a month, you too will be able to play like I do."

At first Abe thought the stranger was fooling with him, and then he realized the bearded golfer was perfectly serious. Abe thanked his new acquaintance, left the golf course, and while driving home made a solemn pledge to attend services every day and to observe the rules of kashruth meticulously for a month. To be able to play like that fellow—it would definitely be worth it.

There was a synagogue only two blocks from Abe's home, and for the next month Abe Friedman attended both morning and evening services. He carefully ingested only kosher food for that same period, and when the month was over he rushed to the golf course, eager to try his hand at a hole in one. As he set the ball down on his tee, he could see the bearded golfer at a distance. Carefully, Abe swung his club, and when he looked down he was shocked, disappointed and angry. He had missed completely. He felt humiliated.

Clutching his club, he ran across the links and caught up with the bearded golfer, who recognized him immediately.

Abe's voice was loud and angry. "Didn't you tell me that I could play like you if I went to shul every day for a month and kept kosher?" he demanded of the yarmulke wearer.

"Yes, yes, I did," he replied.

"Well, it doesn't work! I did everything like you said and it doesn't work."

"Which shul did you go to?"

"Which shul? What difference does it make? I went to the Madison Avenue shul, near my house."

The bearded golfer smiled. "Well, that explains it," he said. "That's the tennis shul."

First the Coffee

An El Al airliner had just taken off from Ben-Gurion Airport near Tel Aviv, bound for Paris. By error the intercom was open, and every word that was uttered in the cockpit could be heard in the passenger section.

A strong voice, presumably that of the pilot, came booming out of the public address system: "Well, now that we're airborne, first I'm going to have a cup of coffee, and then I'm going to find that gorgeous new stewardess and give her a few passionate kisses."

Leah the stewardess heard everything, from the

tail end of the aircraft. She came rushing down the aisle, to warn the pilot that his intercom was open. When she passed the third row, a little old lady called out, "Wait, wait, Leah—let him finish his coffee first."

Special Minister

The early years of Israeli independence and statehood were very difficult. When the State of Israel was proclaimed in May 1948, in accordance with a United Nations resolution authorizing the establishment of a Jewish state, there were 650,000 Jews in the country; within three years, nearly a million impoverished Jews streamed into the country, many of them survivors of the Nazi camps, the others Jews from various Moslem countries.

Of course there was a severe shortage of everything—food, homes, clothing, jobs, schools, hospitals, money. Somehow, with enormous effort and outstanding support from Jewish communities around the world and some help from a few Western countries, things gradually improved. Food rationing, which had been instituted in the early critical years, was ended. Israelis laughingly referred to the crane as their national bird, for wherever one went, the cranes could be seen, helping to put up apartment houses, schools, hospitals, factories.

The story is told of one especially generous American Jewish philanthropist whose financial support was very much appreciated. This individual had made a fortune the hard way, starting out with almost nothing and working himself up to a position where he was said to be worth many scores of millions. Now in his late seventies, he was eager to associate with educated people, with idealists, and with the intellectuals.

One day, following one of his frequent trips to Israel, he said to the then prime minister, David Ben-Gurion, "You know, I don't really deserve it, but I would be so honored if you could appoint me a member of the Israeli Cabinet."

Ordinarily the tough Ben-Gurion would have snorted in response, but the Israeli leader was a realist. He needed this man's ongoing help and goodwill, and the additional financial support that he could bring in. He leaned back in his chair, lost in thought, and then beamed.

"Listen, how would you like to be Minister of Transport and Health?" he asked his American visitor.

The philanthropist was clearly delighted. "It sounds terrific," he said. "What do I have to do?"

"It's simple—you stand at the airport and when the tourists leave, just call out after them, *fohr gezunt*—have a good, healthy trip!"

Fellow Traveler

Scene: A European-style train, with compartments seating six people, three on each side. A Jewish traveler, Gottesman, is alone in a compartment when the train pulls out. He takes off his shoes, rests them on the empty seats near him, spreads out his papers and parcels, and tries to nap. Suddenly, the door opens and a passenger comes in

181

and takes a seat opposite Gottesman. The man is smartly dressed, clean-shaven, and his head is uncovered.

Embarrassed, Gottesman puts his shoes back on, retrieves his papers and parcels and places them in the rack overhead, and sits straight in his seat, like a young pupil in grammar school. He unfolds his Yiddish paper carefully and quietly, and tries to read.

The stranger leans toward him. "Tell me," he says, his accent Oxonian, "when is Yom Kippur this year?"

Gottesman mutters, "Aha!" and proceeds to slip off his shoes and slouch into his seat. He tells the traveler the date, and then puts his feet up on the empty seat.

Bejeweled Martians

In a remote corner of Wisconsin a farmer suddenly came upon a strange-looking creature. He stood four feet tall, was wearing something metallic and green, he had very large ears and two long antennae emerging from his oversize head. A half-dozen necklaces were draped around his neck, and on each of his long fingers he wore three or four rings.

The farmer of course was overcome with awe, but tried to remain calm. "Where you from?" he asked the odd-looking creature.

"Mars," replied the creature in green.

"And do all the Mars people dress like you, with all those rings and necklaces?"

"Oh, no—only the Jews."

"Oy Vay!"

Mrs. Tillie Goldenberg was a snob and a social climber. The wealthier she and her husband became, the more she sought entry into what she considered to be the upper crust of society. Instead of donating funds to her local synagogue and Jewish charities, she began to concentrate her gifts on museums and the local opera company.

When her husband died, she inherited many millions. As soon as she could she moved to a swanky apartment, and changed her name to Theresa Garfield. She took up golf and secretly took elocution lessons. Her great triumph was being invited to join the country club that was restricted to wealthy, white Protestants of Anglo-Saxon origin.

One evening she was dining at the exclusive club, wearing a new and striking gown. A passing waiter accidentally spilled some hot soup over her, causing her to jump up and exclaim in a loud voice, ''Oy vay''—and when she saw the looks of consternation on the faces of the people at her table, she added, ''Whatever that may mean.''

Fair Exchange

Golda Meir, the quintessential Jewish grandmother who became Israel's first woman prime minister, was visiting the White House when Richard Nixon was president. The whole world was still awed by Israel's swift, almost miraculous victory in the Six

Day War, in which the charismatic General Moshe Dayan served as minister of defense.

Nixon, the story goes, said to Golda, "How about a swap? You give us General Dayan and we'll give you two American generals in return."

Golda pondered, smiled, and replied: "Okay, it's a deal—we'll give you General Dayan and you give us General Motors and General Electric."

Godly Gunmen

In an Orthodox neighborhood in Brooklyn, where practically all the Jewish families were Hassidic, it was not unusual to see little boys, aged six or seven, poring over books from early in the morning until late in the evening. These strictly reared children almost never watched television or went to the movies. They lived in a self-contained world of their own, where holiness and religious observance were terms bandied about every day.

Nevertheless, even the children of Hassidim could not totally escape the cultural mores of the time and place they lived in. The story is told of two such Hassidic boys, their sidecurls hanging loosely, the fringes of their *tallit katan* (a special religious garment) visible, playing cops and robbers. One boy is the cop and the other the robber. Both boys point their fingers and hands at each other, as though they are shooting real pistols.

One boy pretends to pump three bullets into his adversary, shouting, "Bang! Bang! You're dead— God forbid!"

Cantorial Plea

The cantor of a prominent synagogue in an affluent area of New York was strolling down Fifth Avenue on a beautiful autumn afternoon. He looked very happy and very satisfied with himself. Suddenly a youngster of perhaps eleven or twelve stopped him, shouting excitedly:

"Cantor! Cantor! Your house is on fire!"

The cantor paused and said to the boy, "How do you know I'm a cantor?"

"I've heard you many times, in the temple. Hurry, hurry, your house is on fire!"

"And how do you know where I live?"

"I know, I know, my mother showed me your house a few times, the red brick on Fifth Avenue near Ninety-first Street."

The cantor was now convinced that the boy was telling the truth. He reached into a pocket, withdrew his tuning fork, struck the curb with the instrument, held it to his ear, and then let go in a strong baritone, "*Gevald!* Help!"

Citrus Squeezer

The scene was a bar in a rough-and-tough area of Brooklyn. A big, burly, and bearded young man who must have weighed at least three hundred pounds was bragging about his ability to take an orange, and with one squeeze reduce it to pulp and juice. He challenged anyone to do as well.

Up stepped a slight, bespectacled man in his

forties, wearing a suit and tie in a place where almost everyone else was dressed in denim overalls and heavy woolen shirts. Without a word he grabbed not an orange from a pile on the bar but a rather large grapefruit, and with one swift squeeze, to everyone's amazement, he squeezed it dry. All the pulp and juice and seeds from the large fruit were now spread out all over the bar. Even the challenger was impressed. He turned to the newcomer and asked him:

"What do you do for a living, friend?"

The scholarly-looking erstwhile squeezer smiled and replied: "I'm a collector for the UJA."

Mexican Password

Louis Abramowitz could not wait to retire. As soon as he could, he drove with his wife, Fanny, to Mexico City, checked into a hotel, and began to tour the usual sights. Louis did not know, until he was in Mexico for a few days, that bullfighting was a popular sport in that city.

On a day that his wife decided to go to the beauty parlor, Louis proceeded to the stadium where the bulls were challenged and fought. He was deeply disappointed to learn that all the seats were sold out. On a hunch, he walked around the large arena, coming upon the side entrance, where he saw various men being allowed to enter when each one called out what seemed to be a secret password. One yelled "Matador," and another called out "Toreador." Louis remembered his brother's

186

name, got into line, walked toward the entrance, and shouted "Isidore!" and was admitted.

Nu, Mr. Diplomat?

When Dag Hammarskjöld was a secretary-general of the United Nations he paid a formal, official visit to Israel and was invited to dinner by Prime Minister David Ben-Gurion. Mrs. Ben-Gurion, known far and wide by her first name, Paula, was a painfully frank and outspoken person. When the U.N. official, a bachelor, was seated next to her at dinner, she lost no time in confronting him.

"Nu," she said to him as other diplomats almost choked on their food. "Why doesn't a nice man like you get married? What's the matter, there are not enough nice unmarried women to choose from?"

The Swedish diplomat's response to Paula is unknown.

Fatherly Advice

A Jewish father is seen driving his young, inquisitive son through the countryside, en route to the Catskills, where the child will be left for a week to vacation with his grandparents.

"Dad, what's the name of that big tree?" the child asks as they speed by an unusual clump of trees.

"I don't know."

They pass a meadow where horses can be seen.

187

"How many years does a horse live, Papa?" the boy asks.

"I don't know."

"What's the name of that pretty bird that just flew by?"

"I don't know."

They drive for a while in silence, until the child speaks up again.

"Dad, can I ask you something?"

"Ask, ask, my son," the father says, "if you don't ask, you'll never learn."

Einstein's Living

Joseph was a freshman in college, and his grandfather, who had come to America from the other side, regarded him with awe and pride. One day he asked his grandson to explain Einstein's theory of relativity.

"Well, *zaide*, it's like this," Joseph said. "Let's say there's a fellow and he had a sweetheart, and they're in a car and there isn't enough room for everyone, so his girlfriend sits on his lap. She sits on his lap for an hour but he doesn't care, to him it feels like a minute. Now, let's say the same fellow accidentally sits on a hot stove—that one minute on the stove feels like an hour. That's relativity."

The grandfather had been listening carefully, nodding his head imperceptibly. Finally, he spoke:

"Tell me, Joseph, from this Einstein makes a living?"

188

Thirsty Traveler

Two elderly Jews were seated in a train compartment. They had entrained at a small town and were now en route to Warsaw, way back in the early 1920s. One of the passengers was carefully reading the popular Yiddish daily, *Haint*. The other passenger, with nothing to read, kept mumbling aloud, "Oy, am I thirsty!" He did this over and over, much to the irritation of his neighbor.

When the train stopped at a small station, the newspaper-reading passenger dashed out of the train, bought a glass of water, and brought it to his neighbor. "Here," he said, "drink."

The other man finished the entire glassful of water in one swallow. He leaned back in his seat, and as the train pulled out, he was heard to mumble aloud, "Oy, was I thirsty!"

Rhythmic Couple

Dr. and Mrs. John MacIntyre were highly successful blacks who owned a large and expensive Park Avenue apartment. Dr. MacIntyre was a top-notch cardiologist and his wife was the provost of a college in New York City. Oddly, they employed an elderly Jewish couple, Sam and Molly Lieberman—Molly was the cook (the MacIntyres entertained quite frequently) and Sam helped her, did the shopping, and helped keep the apartment spotless.

One day Mrs. MacIntyre asked Molly and Sam to prepare a dinner for eight people for the following evening, and to be sure to "make those marvelous gefilte fish"—but from scratch, not from a jar or a can. In the morning, Sam and Molly went shopping; they bought the various kinds of fish and vegetables they would need, and hurried back to their Park Avenue kitchen.

And then they got to work—cleaning the fish, chopping it, mixing it, adding the vegetables and spices, and of course all the while, as they worked through the day, singing. They sang Sabbath songs and festival songs; they sang erstwhile hit songs of the Yiddish stage; they even worked their way into liturgical and Hassidic tunes.

By six-thirty, the aroma of fresh-made gefilte fish wafted through the apartment. Sam and Molly were now putting the finishing touches on what promised to be a culinary delight. They were slicing carrots that would top the gefilte fish portions, and as they worked they continued to sing, happy as a pair of larks.

Mrs. MacIntyre's best friend was also an educator and she had come early, at her friend's request. Both women were now dressed in evening clothes, earrings, rings, bracelets, and necklaces prominently displayed. Mrs. MacIntyre took her friend's hand and together they approached the kitchen. The door was pushed open slightly, and the sweet, pungent aroma of the fish dish and the other components of the meal enveloped the two women, who listened, almost transfixed, as the elderly Jewish couple continued their singsong.

Mrs. MacIntyre turned to her friend, her head pointing to the couple in the kitchen, and said:

"Don't they have rhythm!"

Theater Panner

The Horowitzes were a loving couple, except that she loved to go to the theater, and he avoided it like the plague. Whenever his wife would take in a matinee or an evening performance, Mr. Horowitz would seek out some friends and enjoy a game of gin rummy or pinochle.

Once, however, she put her foot down. She insisted that he accompany her, assuring her husband that the critics had all raved about the new show on Broadway. He relented, sat through the performance, and when they left, Mrs. Horowitz asked her husband what he thought of the play.

"Terrible!" he said. "Just plain terrible!"

"Tell me, come on, just tell me."

"All right. First, he wants, she says no, later she wants, he says no. Then they both want, and the curtain comes down. Nu, this I need?"

Frustrated Comic

One of the happiest events in a Jewish family's life is the ceremony surrounding the circumcision of a newborn infant boy. This generally takes place on the eighth day of the child's life, and the actual rite is usually performed by a *mohel,* a ritual circumciser who in all likelihood learned his special skill from his father, who in turned learned it from his father, and so on.

These men (recently a tiny number of women have also begun to practice this very special vocation, among Reform and Conservative Jews) are in great demand, and often, in the larger urban centers, will do three or four such operations per day. In most cases they explain to the family and friends gathered for the ceremony, and for the reception that usually follows, the religious significance of the event. Some of these men are also frustrated stand-up comics.

One such mohel, wearing a gauze face mask to protect the infant about to be circumcised, liked to say that the mask was there not to protect the child from germ infection, but so that "he shouldn't recognize me when he grows up." Another liked to tell about the British royal family, which for more than four decades has had their male offspring circumcised by a Jewish mohel (without the special blessings reserved for a Jewish child). One day, the now-aging mohel was called to the palace and was told that the royal family wished to honor him for his many years of service.

The British official said, "We will shortly announce that you are to be known as the Oil of Moil (Earl of mohel)."

A Scroll Falls

Every synagogue in the world features the Scroll of the Torah, a rolled-up parchment, hand-inscribed copy of the Pentateuch, the first third of the Jewish Bible. At Sabbath and holiday services the Torah is carried around the congregation, and worshipers extend their hands reverently to touch and kiss the Torah. As a sign of respect, everyone in the congregation remains standing while the Torah is being carried or lifted, before it is replaced in the Holy Ark.

There is also a belief that if the Torah—God forbid!—is dropped, everyone within view of the accident must fast for forty days. No one is sure if this ever happened, and some rabbis will explain that the fast is only during daylight hours, and that it's really a tradition rather than a hard-and-fast rule.

One day, in a Long Island synagogue, during the joyous holiday of Simchat Torah, when all the scrolls are paraded around the congregation, and are danced with and embraced lovingly, an older member of the congregation tripped, slipped, and fell with the Torah he was carrying. There was an immediate hush as people rushed to pick up the Torah and the embarrassed congregant.

"Are you hurt, Nat?" he was asked. "Only my pride" was the old man's quick rejoinder.

Another congregant turned to the rabbi, his tone somewhat challenging. "Well, Rabbi, so are we going to fast forty days?" he asked.

The rabbi looked at his questioner. In a low voice he said: "I didn't see a thing." And the dancing and rejoicing with the Torah scrolls continued unabated.

In Quest of an Orb

A Jewish businessman who had never taken a real vacation decided it was high time he did so. He was now in his sixties, his wife had passed on two years earlier, his children were grown and on their own, and he had not been out of the United States for more than fifty years, when he had arrived in America as a small child, an impoverished immigrant fortunate enough to have departed from Poland on the eve of World War II.

He entered the office of a travel agent and explained that he wished to travel and enjoy a trip overseas but he did not really know where he wanted to go. The woman agent began to hand him some brochures when the phone in her inner office rang.

"Mr. Cohen," he said. "I must take that call. Here's a globe of the world. Why don't you spin it, choose a place you want to go, and we can arrange for you to have a wonderful trip."

Cohen now faced the globe and gave it a twirl. It stopped when his finger touched the Soviet Union. *Pfui,* Cohen thought, as he gave the globe another spin. Who wants to go Russia, home of the Cossacks and pogroms? he mused. The orb of the world turned and turned and when Cohen stopped it, his finger was atop Germany. *Pfui* again, Cohen mused, Germany! Naziland, where they murdered six million Jews! No, thanks! He gave the globe another turn, and when he stopped it, his finger rested on Poland. Poland, he thought to himself, home of the anti-Semites, where once there were three million Jews, and now maybe there are three thousand dying, old people. Thanks but no thanks, he thought.

The travel agent, Mrs. Slawson, emerged from her office, beaming. "Well, have you decided where you want to go?" she asked.

194

Cohen hesitated. In a low, almost inaudible voice he asked, "Maybe you got a different globe?"

New Recipe

Emanual Leibowitz was retired and living in a small Florida town. One afternoon he was seated on the porch of his home when he looked up to see what was causing a terrible smell in the area. All he could see, coming down the road, was a farmer driving a team of horses, with a wagon that seemed to be placed very high. The foul odor, he quickly surmised, must be coming from the wagon.

The elderly retiree stepped into the road. "Good afternoon," he called out to the farmer, and the latter nodded and mumbled, "Afternoon."

"Where you headed?" Leibowitz asked.

"Next town, Millville."

"What's in the wagon?"

"Manure."

Leibowitz was puzzled. He knew the word's meaning, but he had never met anyone involved with it, obviously in some commercial transaction.

"What do you do with the manure?" Leibowitz asked.

"Spread it over strawberries."

Leibowitz pondered for a moment, and then said: "Well, come over sometime for lunch—try it our way. We use sour cream."

A Telegram Arrives

Shapiro and Feinman were partners in the sports-coat business. The bulk of the selling season was usually in late spring and early summer, and here it was mid-August and they were still stuck with ten thousand blue-and-white-checked sports coats that nobody seemed to want to buy. Despondent, the two men were seated in their tiny office off Manhattan's Seventh Avenue when a stranger walked in and introduced himself as a buyer from Argentina.

"You wouldn't by any chance have any blue-and-white-checked sports jackets for sale?" he asked.

Shapiro spoke up first. "Well, we might have a few left," he ventured. "How many can you use?"

"I desperately need ten thousand for one chain of stores all over Latin America."

After some discussion and price haggling, a deal was struck. The Argentinian buyer announced that he was returning to Buenos Aires that evening and would send them a wire within a few days confirming the order, for which, he explained, he needed approval from his superior. "But don't worry," he told the partners, "it's just a formality."

For the next three days, the two men were nervous wrecks. Every time the phone rang, they thought it might be the confirmation being phoned in, but no such call came. Finally, on the fourth day, a messenger from Western Union arrived and handed an envelope to Shapiro. His fingers trembling, Shapiro ripped open the familiar yellow envelope and quickly read the message. He turned to his partner, all smiles: "Sam—it's good news. Your sister died."

Syrian Crisis

Helen Gittleman was a spinsterish secretary who had worked for more than twenty-five years in New York's garment center, whose hub is Seventh Avenue, euphemistically renamed Fashion Avenue. During her vacation one year she traveled to the Far East, and on the way home her plane was routed from India to England, and then Kennedy Airport in New York.

Over Syria, however, the giant airliner developed some engine trouble and the pilot decided to land in Damascus to make a minor repair. All of the passengers were instructed to remain in their seats as the repair was being made; they were also advised that Syrian soldiers might pass through the aisle, checking the passengers.

Suddenly, Helen realized that she was probably the only Jewish passenger on board. She also knew that Syrians did not need any excuse to harass Jews. Thus, after a half hour, when two fierce-looking Syrian soldiers came up to her and asked to see her passport, she was ready for them. Nonchalantly, she handed it over, elated that her trip to Israel a few years earlier had been stamped into her earlier passport, which was now expired.

One of the soldiers spoke up: "What religious persuasion are you, madam?" he asked. Almost sweetly, Helen Gittleman replied, "Oh, I'm a Sev-

197

enth Avenue Adventist.'' The passport was handed back, and the rest of the journey was uneventful.

A Teen's Proposal

The regular, often daily study of the Talmud is believed by many to be a sure path to sharp-mindedness. The great sages of the Talmud enjoyed the mental challenge of *pilpul*—the casuistic taking apart of an accepted statement or belief and turning it this way and that so that every possible perspective and facet could be ascertained. Take the story of a father and his son.

The young man, now in his teens, approaches his father and asks for a raise in his weekly allowance.

''What for?'' his father asks.

''Well, I'd like to go to night school.''

''And if you go to night school, then what?''

''Well, I'll get a better job.''

''Nu, so what if you get a better job?''

''Well, then I'll buy new clothes and go to nice places.''

''All right, so you buy new clothes and go to nice places. And then what?''

''Well, I'll meet a wonderful, beautiful girl.''

''So, you meet a beautiful girl. So what?''

''So, I'll marry her.''

''All right, you meet this girl, you get married. Nu, what then?''

''Well, then I'll be very happy!''

''So all right, you're happy. And then what?''

Priestly Request

Joseph Kaplan had always wanted to be a *ko'hane*, a member of the ancient priestly family whose members in the days of the Holy Temple were charged with conducting the special religious services in Jerusalem, and who, in modern times, were considered a notch above the Levites (their helpers) and certainly on a higher rung than the ordinary Israelites. When the Scroll of the Torah is read aloud in the synagogue on the Sabbath or holidays, it is a *ko'hane* who is called first to inaugurate the reading.

Kaplan approached his rabbi one day. "Rabbi," he said, "I want you to make me a *ko'hane*."

The rabbi tried to be gentle. "Sorry, Joe, I can't make you one. It can't be done."

Kaplan persisted. "My thanks will be expressed in the form of a ten-thousand-dollar gift to the synagogue."

The rabbi laughed, and adamantly refused. A month later Kaplan cornered the rabbi again. "Twenty-five thousand," Kaplan said. "Make me a *ko'hane*." Again a month passed, and again the rabbi was accosted by Kaplan. "Okay, fifty grand," Kaplan called out. The rabbi took Kaplan by the arm and seated him on a bench in the sanctuary. "I can't do it, Joe," he said. "That's final, but tell me, for heaven's sake, why do you want to be a *ko'hane* so much?"

"Because my father was one, and so was my grandfather."

No Ticket, No Service

The overwhelming majority of synagogues allow everyone who wishes to attend a service to do so, without charge of course. (There may be a charge for lecture and similar programs, but never for daily or Sabbath or holiday services.) Except for the High Holy Days, the ten-day period from Rosh Hashanah to Yom Kippur. Since the upkeep of synagogues (outside Israel) is voluntary, this is the one time of year when members and nonmembers are expected to buy tickets to join the special services. The funds derived often go a long way to maintaining the institution for a whole year.

Thus, one lovely September day, a young college student appeared at a suburban synagogue outside Philadelphia on the morning of the first day of Rosh Hashanah. A uniformed guard stopped him. "Gotta ticket?" he asked.

The young man explained that he had just arrived from out of town and wanted to see his father, who was inside, to get the key to the family home. The guard was stubborn; no ticket, no admission. The collegian argued that all he wanted was to see his father, get the key, and then he'd be off. The guard relented.

"All right," he said, allowing the young man to enter the temple. "But no praying!"

Japanese and Jews

Whether the following story is true or apocryphal, only historians know, but many people believe it happened just as it is remembered.

A community of Hassidic Jews, escaping from the Nazis in the early years of World War II, when the Hitler-Stalin pact was still in force, managed to reach the Japanese port city of Kobe, awaiting transportation by sea to the United States. While in Kobe, where they were aided by the minuscule Jewish community—many of whose members were refugees from the 1917 Bolshevik revolution—the Japanese attack on Pearl Habor took place, and the Jews realized they were stuck in Kobe for the duration. They tried to keep a low profile, spending their time in study and prayer, and awaiting deliverance.

The Germans and Japanese, of course, were allies, and somehow the Nazis learned of the Jews in Kobe. They demanded of their Japanese partners that the Kobe Jewish community be rounded up and imprisoned and eventually executed. The Japanese, however, were reluctant to carry out their ally's wishes. The Germans continued to apply pressure on the Japanese, and finally, sometime in 1942 or 1943, the rabbi of the Hassidic community found himself in Tokyo, seated in a room in the headquarters building of the ministry of defense.

He was a medium-size gentleman in his fifties, wearing a small yarmulke on his head, occasionally stroking his long, white beard. If he was frightened he did not show it. He sat at one side of a long

201

table, facing eight or ten high Japanese military officials, all of them in full uniform, medals and ribbons adorning their chests. At one end of the table sat an interpreter.

Finally, the head of the Japanese group looked squarely at the rabbi, whose black hat rested on his lap. "Tell me," the Japanese said, "why do our friends the Germans hate you Jews so much?" The interpreter translated the question, averting his eyes from the rabbi.

Without hesitation, the Hassidic rabbi responded: "Because, sir, like you, we are Asians." The interpreter translated, the Japanese officials looked confused, then they seemed to whisper to one another, and finally the group's leader told the rabbi he was free to go and return to Kobe.

After the end of World War II the Hassidic community continued its interrupted journey to the United States, where they established new schools of religious learning.

Meeting on a Beach

The locale is Florida in the winter months. Sun worshipers are enjoying the warmth and relaxed atmosphere of the beach. Mrs. Perlman, who was widowed two years earlier, is a devotee of the beach, where she comes almost daily, bringing her tanning lotion, a light sandwich, and a romantic novel. Although she is not a forward person, she certainly would not mind meeting an eligible bachelor, and perhaps even marrying again. Life alone is so lonely!

On this particular day, after she had spread out her blanket and made herself comfortable, Mrs. Perlman noticed a new man not more than four feet away. He has obviously just covered himself with suntan lotion and is trying to get some color and look more Floridian. She cannot help but notice that he is unusually pale.

As though responding to a friend's dare, she clears her throat and says to the stranger:

"Excuse me, you're new here?"

He opens his eyes, stares at Mrs. Perlman for a moment, and then closes his eyes again.

"Yeah," he replies.

She waits, having already noted that he seems to be about the right age for a woman of her years, and that his left hand does not sport a wedding band.

"So how come you're so pale?" she persists.

Without even opening his eyes, the stranger replies: "I've been in jail for thirty years."

Mrs. Perlman takes a little time to absorb this tidbit. She continues her questioning:

"What happened?"

"I killed my wife," the man says, never even moving from his supine position or opening his eyes.

Again Mrs. Perlman takes time to absorb this information. And again she continues:

"So—that means you're a single man now?"

Breaking the Law

Although there is said to be in Israel a former American Indian who converted to Judaism and became a strictly observant Hassid, there do not seem to be many Indians who became Jewish. The story is told nevertheless about one such Indian who was now a Jew, married to a Jewish woman and living with her somewhere on the plains of Nebraska. One day this fellow leaves the family tepee to go out and hunt for buffalo. He rides out early in the day, soon after the sun rises, and after an hour or so, deep in an isolated ravine, he spots his quarry, a big, strong buffalo. He dismounts from his horse, sneaks up behind the huge animal, and with his trusty tomahawk kills the buffalo with one powerful blow to the animal's neck.

As he prepares to drag the carcass home on a makeshift cart, he suddenly panics. Although he is alone in the deserted area, he talks aloud to the trees and rocks that surround him.

"Oy vay!" he yells. "Shirley will kill me! I used a dairy tomahawk."

Premature Obituary

The *Jewish Chronicle* is a revered Jewish-interest weekly newspaper that is published in London and read by virtually every British Jewish family, as well as by many Jews on the Continent and in Israel.

Two friends, Maurice Cohen and Harry Goldberg, had been getting the paper for many, many years. Now both men were retired and both had been widowed. They lived alone and saw each other several times a week. In recent years, both had developed a new habit—whenever they picked up a newspaper, they found themselves turning to the obituary column first.

One Friday morning, Maurice opened his *Chronicle,* turned to the obituary notices, and was startled, to say the least, to see his own obituary prominently displayed. He realized it was an error, but the appearance of the news item shocked him. With trembling fingers he pressed the numbers of his friend Harry's phone, and when Harry said hello, Maurice said:

"Have you gotten the *J.C.* this morning?"

"Yes, it just came. Haven't opened it yet."

"Do me a favor, turn to page forty-seven. Read the story in the third column."

Through the telephone wires came the sound of pages being turned, and then a moment or two of silence, and finally Harry spoke up:

"Maurice, from where are you calling?"

Famous Diamond

The annual major fund-raising dinner for the United Jewish Appeal campaign in town had just gotten under way in the poshest ballroom in the best hotel. Everyone who was anyone was there, dressed in their finery, ready to announce large gifts to the campaign to help fellow Jews in need all over the world.

A newcomer in town, Harold Blum, was seated at a table with a dozen other people, including one woman who seemed to be alone. She was elegantly dressed, and on her left hand, third finger, wore a diamond ring that to Blum looked as big as a golf

205

ball. The newcomer could not take his eyes off it, and finally said to the woman, "Forgive me for staring, but I have never seen a diamond so beautiful, or so large. Is it famous?"

The woman smiled. "Yes, yes, it's famous all right," she said. "It's called the Polofsky diamond."

"Really? Is it cursed or anything, I mean, does it have a story?"

"Oh, yes, it definitely is cursed."

"How?"

"It comes with Mr. Polofsky."

A General and a Student

Learning and education are lifetime goals for most Jews. From the time a Jewish child is old enough to read, his parents seek to encourage him or her to pursue a scholastic life. Many rabbis have had the experience of addressing a congregation or an audience, and afterward someone will approach— often a highly successful and affluent businessman—and boast about his father or grandfather or uncle. And inevitably the boast will be to the effect that his relative or progenitor was a rabbi or a scholar or perhaps a cantor. If that person was merely rich and successful, it was usually not a point of pride.

The story is told of a shtetl in the nineteenth century, where the Jews lived very poor lives but continued to pursue biblical and Talmudic studies. One day, in this particular shtetl, there was a parade of the local army company. Classes in the religious

206

school were suspended for the day, and everyone came out to watch, as the soldiers came trooping by, rifles on their shoulders, marching smartly, accompanied by a marching band composed of drummers and trumpeters. And then came the general, seated on a tall white horse, the two of them bedecked with ribbons, the general resplendent in a gold uniform, epaulettes gleaming, his face beaming with pride, sporting a big, shiny sword.

A father held his young son's hand as the general went by on his horse. The boy couldn't have been more than seven. As the rhythm of the drums filled the air and the blare of the trumpets enveloped everyone, the father said to his child: "You see the general, Moshe? If you don't study, you'll wind up just like him!"

"I Didn't Do It!"

A supervisor from the city's Board of Jewish Education was paying a rare visit to one of the newer Jewish religious schools in town. He was well aware of the fact that getting trained, qualified teachers was the principal problem facing the city's Jewish schools.

The class of nine-year-olds waited politely as their teacher introduced the visitor, explaining that the supervisor wished to pose a few questions.

"Who knocked down the walls of Jericho?" the supervisor asked.

There was total silence and no response whatsoever. The visitor pointed to one bright-looking student in the front row.

The youngster stiffened and said, "I didn't do it."

Puzzled, the supervisor turned to the teacher.

"If he says he didn't do it," the teacher said, "he didn't do it—he's very trustworthy."

Shocked, the supervisor went to the rabbi and reported the exchange in class. The rabbi listened carefully, stroked his beard a few times, and then picked up the phone, explaining that he was calling the president of the congregation, whom he described as "a very generous man." The rabbi then proceeded to tell the synagogue's president of what had transpired, and listened intently as the congregational leader talked. Finally, smiling happily, the rabbi hung up and turned to the supervisor.

"I told you he's very generous," the rabbi said. "He said we should have it repaired, and send the bill to him."

California Bound

Moses was known to have a stuttering problem. One biblical commentator insists that God asked the great Lawgiver to choose a homeland for the Jewish people. And when Moses responded, he stammered: "Ca-Ca-Ca-" and God finished the word for him. "Okay, Canaan it is," the Lord said. According to this commentator, Moses was trying to enunciate the word *California*.

Boating Tip

This story took place thousands of years ago, when slavery was in full swing. Somewhere off the coast of Israel there was a large ship, propelled by slaves chained to long oars. Urging them on to ever-greater feats of rowing was their harsh taskmaster, who used a whip to ensure that the oarsmen did not slow down the steady rhythm of the ship's movement. One of the slaves was a Hebrew by the name of Lemuel. Like all the other slaves, he rowed as hard as he could, and despite his best efforts, he felt the lash of the whip on his back several times a day.

Finally, after some twelve hours of steady rowing, a new crew was being put in place, the exhausted and lashed crewmembers ready to fall onto their straw pallets belowdecks. But not Lemuel; he approached the deck officer with a request to see the captain.

The officer on that particular day was in a good mood. He pointed to the bridge above, where a burly man stood, his eyes fixed ahead. "Go ahead," Lemuel was told. Diffidently, the Hebrew slave approached the bridge, bowing and scraping all the way, awaiting the captain's nod that would indicate he could speak. Finally the captain nodded, and Lemuel said:

"O mighty captain of the seas, I have but one request of you, grand sir," the slave said. "I am new on this glorious vessel, and indeed this is my maiden voyage on the Great Sea. Pray, tell me, kind sir, how much should I tip the whipper?"

Slow Learner

A wealthy man hired a private tutor for his son, who was a slow learner. The tutor's job was to instruct the youngster in Jewish studies. One day the father was standing at the doorway of the room in which his son was being taught, and was startled to hear his son learning the kaddish, the mourner's prayer, generally recited for a newly deceased parent.

He confronted the tutor. "Why are you teaching him the kaddish? I'm still very much alive."

"Don't worry, sir. It will be at least one hundred years before he learns it."

Real Bargain

Shnorrer is a Yiddish word usually translated as beggar. The translation is inadequate. A real shnorrer regards himself as a member of a respectable vocation. In Tel Aviv, for example, there are certain beggars who operate only in certain streets. It is not unusual for a storekeeper on one of those streets to receive a postcard during the summer, announcing that the shnorrer is on vacation that week and that he expects double when he returns the following week.

One shnorrer managed to wangle an appointment with one of the Rothschild barons. "Sir," he said to the multimillionaire, "I have a wonderful way in which you can save a half-million francs."

"Really?" the Rothschild scion said. "All right, tell me, how?"

"Well, I read in the paper that you will soon marry off your oldest daughter—I'm sure your dowry to the lucky young man will be one million francs."

"So?"

"So, save yourself a half-million—I'll marry her for a half-million."

Parking Solution

Irving Rosenstein is a successful businessman in Florida who enjoys driving around in a big, showy Cadillac. On the eve of a long vacation trip he and his wife are taking overseas, he tells his friend Sam that he just came back from the office of a local finance company, where he borrowed twenty-five dollars. "And I have to pay them two dollars and twenty-five cents a month interest for the loan," he adds.

Sam is startled. "Are you nutty? What are you borrowing twenty-five dollars for?"

"You don't understand," Irving responds. "To get the loan I had to leave my Caddy as collateral. So tell me, where else can I park that monster of mine for two twenty-five a month?"

Gave at the Office

Hyman Markowitz flies to Switzerland and goes skiing, a sport he recently mastered in the upper reaches of New York State. Sure enough, on his first day out in the incredible Alps, he gets lost. A search party is sent out to find him. The searchers call out for him continuously, and the name "Markowitz" is bounced off the mountains for three days. On the third day, Markowitz, whose leg was broken in a fall, is able to hear the voices and echoes coming closer. Finally, he gathers his strength to respond to the call that is reverberating through the Alps. He yells back, "If you're the UJA, I gave already—at the office."

Knowledge Better?

An old Yiddish adage teaches: Better than riches is knowledge.

To which a Jewish wit responds: All of us should be as knowledgeable as Rothschild.

Brief Prayer

A town pauper was in the synagogue on Sabbath morning. Everyone rose to recite the Amidah prayer, which can take as much as eight or ten minutes to complete. From his stance near the Holy Ark the rabbi noticed that the pauper rose for the prayer, said something very rapidly, and then sat down, while everyone else was still going through the entire service.

Later, as people filed out to go home, the rabbi stopped the pauper and asked how it was possible for him to recite the prayers so quickly.

The pauper replied: "Rabbi, with all due respect—you have a nice home, with dishes and furniture and clothes, and a wife and children, a horse and wagon. Me? What have I got in this world? A nagging wife, a couple of crying babies, and an old goat. I live in a hovel. So when I get up to pray, it takes a second or two—I just say, 'Wife, babies, goat' and then I sit down."

Misery Compared

Two lifetime friends, Moe and Joe, meet in the street. Both men look dejected. Moe starts to bemoan his fate:

"Oy, life is terrible! May was a disaster, we never had such a month. I thought it was the end until June came, and June was worse! And July, oy vay, July was the pits. Not one lousy, single sale! Not one."

Joe interrupts. "Listen, everything you say, it's all nonsense," he says. "My wife has cancer, my daughter is getting a divorce, my son was just arrested for smuggling drugs—what could be worse?"

"What? I'll tell you what! August."

Mathematics

Sam chose the winning lottery number, forty-nine, and was awarded five thousand dollars. His friend asked him why he chose forty-nine. "I saw six sevens jumping in my dream, six times seven is forty-nine," he said.

"No, it's forty-two."

"Okay, okay, you be the big-shot mathematician."

"Good Luck"

A poorly paid cantor in a small congregation in the old country was happy to learn that one of his daughters would marry soon. However, he had no money for her dowry, and he approached the congregational leaders, asking for an advance against his salary, a total of two hundred rubles to be deducted from his wages during the next five years.

The congregation's board met and agreed, and called in the cantor to notify him of the decision. A proud man, the cantor said to the board: "I accept your kind offer—but you must understand that if I live another five years, that's your good luck, but if I die before this debt is paid off, nu, that's my good luck!"

No Credit

The word *shnorrer* has become part of the modern idiom. Traditionally, a Jewish shnorrer has an aura of dignity, even a touch of arrogance sometimes associated with independent waiters in Jewish restaurants.

The story is told of a shnorrer who came to the big city and rang the bell of an affluent Jewish home. When the lady of the house opened the door and heard the beggar's plea for charity, she explained that she had no money in the house, but suggested he return the next day.

"No, no," the shnorrer said. "I've already lost a fortune by extending credit."

Rightful Heir

Two brothers, both shnorrers, used to visit Baron Rothschild on the last day of the month, and each would receive fifty francs. One day, one of the brothers died, and when the other turned up for his end-of-the-month remuneration, he was handed the usual fifty francs.

"Wait a minute," he protested to Rothschild's secretary. "I should get twice that!"

"But your brother is dead."

"So, who is the rightful heir, me or Rothschild?"

Mannerly Solution

Many yeshivas (religious schools) employ people as collectors: they solicit funds from affluent people who wish to see the schools maintained. These collectors are generally observant Jews, and some are even ordained rabbis.

One day two such men found themselves invited to lunch at the home of a wealthy philanthropist. Although all three men knew that there was an element of competition involved, since the collectors represented two different yeshivas, each of which insisted that its educational approach was the only correct one, nevertheless lunch was held in a friendly, even convivial atmosphere.

As the meal neared its end, the host was called away to a phone. The meal had been splendid, and there now remained on a plate two lone cookies, a very large one and a rather puny one. Each of the two men wished to grab the bigger of the two cookies, but good manners held them back.

Finally, one of the two, Reb Melech, grabbed the larger of the two desserts, and in two or three swift bites devoured it. The other man, Reb Shimon, berated him: "Feh!" he said. "I'm surprised at you, where are your manners? That was not nice!"

"Wait a minute—if I didn't grab that cookie, what would have happened? You would have offered me the tray, and I would have taken it then, leaving you with the small one, right?"

"Yes, I suppose so."

"So—what are you complaining about?"

So Stay Home!

The town of Chelm in Poland was known as a community where very simpleminded Jews lived. Two Chelmites were once talking. "If I take a horse and wagon and drive to Plonsk, it will take four hours," one said.

"Yes, that's right," his friend replied.

"So if I take four horses and a wagon, I'll get there in no time."

"Right again—so why bother going?"

Unkosher Smoker

A mental patient who was confined to an institution in Connecticut argued for weeks that she be given strictly kosher food. After some time the necessary arrangements were made and the young woman was served only kosher food.

One Saturday afternoon, her counselor, who was also Jewish, came upon her as she was seated in a comfortable lounge chair, smoking one cigarette after another. She confronted her patient: "Hey, how come you demand kosher food, but on the Sabbath, here you are smoking away like a chimney?"

The young woman patient, between puffs, replied, "Well, you know, after all, I'm *meshuggah* (crazy)."

"That's Living!"

Two elderly friends offer each other condolences on the occasion of the passing of a mutual friend, whose funeral they just attended. They are standing outside the funeral parlor on Manhattan's Madison Avenue, where they just witnessed an elegant rabbi deliver a moving eulogy, and where there was standing room only for the mourners and for those who came to pay their last respects to the decedent.

One of the friends, Abramowitz, smiles at the other and says, gesturing toward the funeral chapel, "That's what I call living!"

Doctors First

The adult education class of the synagogue is discussing the Ten Commandments. The teacher asks, "Who is more important—a doctor or a banker?" Mr. Epstein shouts out his answer, "A doctor." The teacher asks, "Why?" And Epstein replies:

"Because 'Thou shall not kill' comes ahead of 'Thou shall not steal.'"

Mother's Prayer

A widowed Jewish mother in the old country had two sons, each of whom had a separate retail business—one sold clothing for the winter season, and the other had a store that specialized in summer garments. Consequently, one son was always praying, when in synagogue, for cold weather, and the other always appealed to the Creator for warm weather.

This left their mother in a quandary until she finally figured out a solution. Prayer book in hand, she would pray for a "warm frost."

Too Much Sleep

A day after the itinerant Jewish preacher—known as a *maggid*—had delivered a fiery talk at the village's synagogue, a congregant met him in the marketplace.

"Rabbi," the congregant said, "after your talk yesterday, I could not sleep all night."

"Really? My talk had such a strong effect on you?"

"No, no, it's just that if I sleep during the day I can never sleep at night too."

"Best Man"

When David Ben-Gurion was the prime minister of Israel he depended heavily on his minister of labor, Golda Meir. Later, Mrs. Meir was appointed foreign minister. Whenever a visitor would ask Ben-Gurion how it was to work with a woman in the Israeli cabinet, he would smile and say: "She's the best man I've got in the whole cabinet!"

Relative Distance

Three Jewish refugees who had succeeded in fleeing Nazi Germany in 1938 reached the Paris office of the Jewish rescue-and-relief agency, the Joint Distribution Committee. All three men looked tired and in need of succor. The JDC man asked the first man, "Where do you want to go?"

"London," he replied. To the same question the second man responded, "Rome." And the third refugee said, "South Africa."

The JDC looked at the third man and asked him: "Why so far?"

The exhausted, uprooted Jew answered: "Far? Far from where?"

Bachelor's Life

Two friends were in a bar talking. Abe was happily married, had two children, and felt sorry for his old buddy, Sam, who was still a bachelor. Sam insisted, however, that the single state was true bliss. Sam proclaimed: "I believe in the Constitution—we Americans are entitled to life, liberty, and the happiness of pursuit. And I also support the bachelor's Golden Rule—Wine, Women, and So long!"

Abe remained unconvinced. He reflected on his friend's words. "You can put that another way," Abe said. "A bachelor owns a car, two suits, he has three girlfriends, and a dozen all-night parking tickets."

Rich and Poor

Two old friends, Morris and Irving, who had known each other for most of their lives, were sitting in a park in Florida. Morris said:

"Do you divide the world into rich and poor, or do you try to get at a man's true character?"

"Well, I do and I don't. I mean, sure, I notice if there are two men, if one is rich and the other is poor. I try not to let that interfere with my judgment. The only time it really does, I have to confess, is if the other fellow is rich and I'm the poor one. That hurts!"

What's Ten Years?

Seymour Goldman was a forty-year-old widower when he married Susan Schwartz, a twenty-year-old nurse. Some people looked askance at the new couple, and once, when Seymour's closest friend raised the issue of the great difference in age, he replied: "It depends on how you look at it. You see, when I look at my wife, I feel ten years younger, and when she looks at me, she feels ten years older. So, it's like we're thirty!"

Late Arrival

Morton Seligman arrived for work one day at nine-thirty, a half hour late. His boss, Mr. Fenster, was furious. "You should have been here at nine!" he shouted. Undaunted, Seligman replied as he hung up his coat, "Why? What happened at nine?"

Overdue Mazel Tov

An elderly Jew visits the office of the congregational burial society. He sits down with the aging secretary, who asks what she can do for him.

"I wish to make arrangements for my wife's interment," he says.

"What are you talking about? We buried her a year ago!"

"No, no, that was my first wife. I got married again."

"You did? I didn't know, so mazel tov!"

221

Bankruptcy Ploy

The guests are arriving at the synagogue for the wedding. The bride is in the bridal room, primping, and the groom is with his parents, nervous but ready for the wedding ceremony. Contrary to all customs, the bride leaves her chamber and approaches the groom, indicating that she wants to be alone with him for a moment.

"Sam, I have to tell you, before we get married," she says, "I've just found out that my father is bankrupt, he just announced chapter eleven."

"I knew it! I knew your father would do anything to stop the wedding," the groom said.

Million Pants?

In most synagogues in the world the daily afternoon service, known as *mincha,* and the evening service, called *ma'ariv,* are usually held in the twilight hours, so that both can be recited together. Often, in the few minutes between the two services, worshipers will find a moment to *shmoos,* best translated as engage in light talk or banter.

In one such synagogue in Philadelphia two old friends were shmoosing, and very often their conversation dealt with rich people and paupers. Said one worshiper: "Look at this fellow, Aaron, the rich man. Thirty years ago he came to this town with one pair of torn pants—and now he has a million."

"What? Is he nutty? What does he need a million pairs of torn pants for?"

Eternal Love

Abe meets his friend Joe, whom he hasn't seen in more than forty years.

Abe: "I've been married to the same woman for thirty years and I'm still in love with the same woman. If my wife ever finds out, she'll kill me."

Bonnet on Bee

Two bees were buzzing along; suddenly they came upon the town's synagogue. One of the bees paused in midtrip, took out a yarmulke, and put it on its tiny head. The other bee, dumbfounded, asked what his friend was doing.

"I don't want to be mistaken for a WASP," the bee with the yarmulke said, and flew off.

Mother in Dark

Question: How many Jewish mothers does it take to screw in a bulb?

Answer: None. When the light goes out, they usually say, "It's all right—I'll just sit in the dark."

Upset Cantor

The cantor came home from the Sabbath services looking upset. His wife asked him what was wrong, but he didn't say anything until after they had finished lunch.

Finally, he articulated the words that were bothering him. "The shamash, the sexton, says, right to my face, that my voice is gone and that I can't sing anymore."

The cantor's wife snorts. "Nonsense! What does he know, that simpleton," she says, trying to console her husband. "What does he know about music and singing? All he does is repeat what everyone in the congregation says!"

Beards and Horses

English money, in the early years of the twentieth century, had engraved on one coin a splendid picture of Queen Victoria astride a handsome horse, and on another coin was pictured King Edward, who wore a thick beard.

Until they learned English, many of the early Jewish immigrants to the British Isles used to hand some coins to their children and say in Yiddish: "Here, take a few horses (*ferd*) and a few beards (*berd*) and buy some milk and bread."

Two Tablets

A wit once wondered why the Ten Commandments were inscribed on two tablets. His friend, Irving, knew the answer without having to think about it.

"See? God first offered the Ten Commandments to the Germans—they said, What do you mean, no killing? Forget it. Then God offered them to the French, and they said, What do you mean, no adultery? Forget it. Then God offered them to the Jews. They said, How much does it cost? And God said, It's free. So they said, We'll take two."

Loyal Reader

The Nazi Party's chief organ was the notorious *Der Sturmer,* a newspaper that charged Jews in Germany with the most heinous crimes. One day, Herr Goldfarb was seated in a Berlin park, reading the Nazi sheet. His secretary came upon him and expressed surprise at his reading matter. Goldfarb explained: "When I read this rag, it says we Jews own the banks, we're in charge of the arts, in fact we're taking over the world; nu, it sounds good. When I read the Jewish paper, only pogroms, troubles, problems. That's why I read *Der Sturmer!*"

Two Samples

Moses Montefiore was one of the greatest Jewish philanthropists of all time. He lived in England during the nineteenth century, and all his life strove to defend endangered Jewish communities and to support religious, educational, and charitable institutions. Once at a dinner party he found himself seated next to a British aristocrat, who was talking about his recent trip to the Far East.

"Did you know," this gentleman said to Montefiore, "that in Japan there are no pigs and no Jews."

Montefiore responded immediately: "Well, then, if you and I go there, Japan will have a sample of each."

Neighborly Slap

The late Sam Levenson, a teacher-turned-comic, liked to tell the one about the Jewish mother who never laid a hand on her son, Daniel, and who was shocked to discover that her son's teacher was known as a slapper. She sat down and wrote a note to the teacher. "If Daniel does not behave himself," the note said, "please don't hit him—slap the boy next to him. He'll get the idea!"

Meet the Daughter

Max: "My new partner wants everything that he sees."

Sol: "Good. Introduce him to my daughter."

Politicians First

Three friends—a surgeon, an architect, and a politician—are on a fishing trip together, on the Sea of Galilee in Israel. While their fishing rods are in the water awaiting the arrival of some fish the men are arguing good-naturedly as to whose profession is the world's oldest.

The surgeon says: "Didn't God make Eve from Adam's rib? Surgery is the oldest calling."

The architect says: "No, before that there was chaos and it took an architect to bring about some order in the world."

The politician says: "You're both wrong. In order to have chaos, first you needed a politician!"

Ushers and Jews

An elderly German Jew was walking down a main street in Berlin in the middle 1930s, before the outbreak of World War II and after the Nazis came to power. A band of young Nazis surrounded him and knocked him to the sidewalk.

One of the Germans shouted at the injured Jew, "Who was responsible for the Germans' defeat in 1918?"

And the old Jew immediately shot back, "The Jews—and the theater ushers."

The Nazis looked at one another, confused. One of them asked, "Why the ushers?"

And the Jew replied, "Why the Jews?"

Surprise Gift

Fred Feigenbaum walks into a stationery store and tells the sales clerk he wants to buy his wife a birthday present, a new pen.

"A little surprise, eh?" the clerk says.

"A big surprise! She's expecting a Cadillac."

Papal Measure

Michael Steinberg is a New York men's suit manufacturer. Many of his employees are of Italian extraction, and after some urging he finally makes his first visit to Italy. His best friend takes him out to lunch after he returns from Rome.

"So, how was the trip?" the friend asks.

"Great. I saw museums, churches—terrific. I even got to meet the Pope."

"Really? So, tell me something about him."

"Well, I figure he's a thirty-nine, short."

Name Exchange

Moses Mendelssohn, an honored philosopher who lived in Germany in the eighteenth century, and whose appearance was unmistakably Jewish, accidentally bumped into a uniformed Prussian officer while he was taking a walk on a Berlin street.

The militaristic Prussian yelled at him, "Swine!"

At which point the philosopher bowed and responded gently, "Mendelssohn," and departed.

Breaking News

A tough sergeant in the Israeli army finds it hard to pass on bad news to his young recruits. One day he is informed that young Michael Abramowitz's mother had a heart attack and died.

The sergeant assembles his men. "At ease," he barks at them. "All those whose mother is living, take a step forward. You, Abramowitz, take a step back."

Important Book

At an English-for-adults class, the teacher asked his students what book they would call the most important. Mrs. Cohen raised her hand. "My checkbook," she replied.

Hardly Recognizable

The Polish city of Chelm has become known in Jewish folklore as a community of naive, silly, dim-witted, but lovable people. The story is told of a Chelmite who is visiting the capital, Warsaw, and spies an old friend, Zalman the chimney sweep, whom he has not set eyes on for many years.

Yudel, the Chelmite, stares at his friend, bewildered. "Oy, vay," he yells at him, "how you've changed!" The other man tries to speak, but the Chelmite continues:

"You used to be big and strong, and now look at you! And your shock of black hair, all gone!

Have you been ill? I don't know how I even recognized you—"

"Listen," the man finally managed to interject,
"I'm not Zalman."

The Chelmite turned ashen. "Oy, oy," he said,
"you've even changed your name."

Scary Lecture

An Israeli astronomer was giving a talk in a Mid-
west synagogue. He asserted that "many of us
believe that the sun will probably die in five billion
years."

From a front row Mrs. Greenspan called out:
"How many years did you say?"

The lecturer responded, "Five billion."

"Oh, thank God—I thought you said five million," Mrs. Greenspan said.

Audience Response

One of the most popular Jewish lecturers in the
United States a number of years ago was the author
Maurice Samuel. Whenever he spoke he drew capacity audiences. Sometimes the public-address
systems did not function properly, and this caused
him distress.

One evening he was giving a lecture in a large
synagogue in Manhattan. People in the last rows
could not hear very well, because the PA system
had broken down, although Samuel raised his voice
as much as possible. One particular gentleman in

the audience, seated in the last row, kept yelling, in Yiddish, *hecher, hecher* (higher or louder). After a few minutes of this man's yells, Samuel stopped his talk, grabbed a chair on the platform, stood up on it, and shouted at the man in the last row: "Okay, okay? High enough for you?"

Hitler's Tonsils

An elderly Jew, in the 1940s, stepped into Macy's to buy some underwear for his wife. He found himself surrounded by chattering women, holding on to bras, slips, and panties, and he felt embarrassed. A salesgirl asked what he wanted, and when he said he wanted to buy a very fancy bra for his wife, the saleswoman asked the size. Now he was stumped. He thought for a moment and finally said, "They're big, very big," obviously referring to his wife's bosom.

"How big?" the clerk persisted. Now the elderly man felt himself blushing.

"How big? Hitler's tonsils should be so big!" he replied.

Sahara Forest

Asher Rabinowitz did not look like a typical lumberjack. He was short and wiry, and when he applied for a job in a remote, wooded area of Washington state the foreman asked him to show his ability. Asher approached a tall, sturdy tree, and to everyone's amazement, with two swings of his ax, the tree came down. He was hired on the spot.

"Tell me," the foreman asked, "where did you learn to cut trees like that?"

Rabinowitz smiled. "In the Sahara Forest," he replied.

"You mean the Sahara Desert."

Asher smiled. "Yeah, that's what they call it now, after I left."

If you have enjoyed
this book in large print
and would like to
receive information
on other books of
Jewish interest,
please send your name to:

Nina Rose
Walker and Company
720 Fifth Avenue
New York, NY 10019